WESTERN WASHINGTON AND OREGON

In Bloom

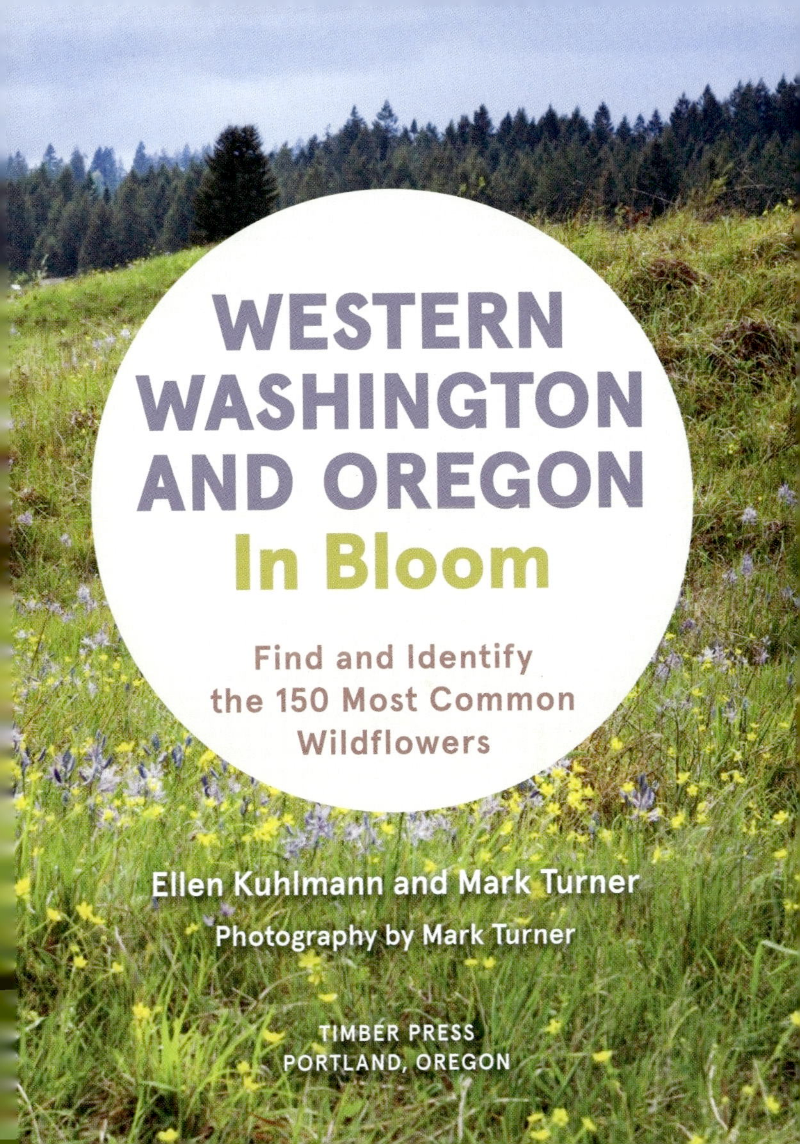
WESTERN
WASHINGTON
AND OREGON
In Bloom
Find and Identify
the 150 Most Common
Wildflowers
Ellen Kuhlmann and Mark Turner
Photography by Mark Turner
TIMBER PRESS
PORTLAND, OREGON

Timber Press
Workman Publishing
Hachette Book Group, Inc.
1290 Avenue of the Americas
New York, New York 10104

timberpress.com

Timber Press is an imprint of Workman Publishing, a division of Hachette Book Group, Inc. The Timber Press name and logo are registered trademarks of Hachette Book Group, Inc.

Printed in Dongguan, China, (TLF) on responsibly sourced paper

Text layout by Mary Velgos, based on series design by Hillary Caudle
Cover design by Leigh Kaisen

Endpaper illustration by Alan Bryan

ISBN 978-1-64326-371-7

A catalog record for this book is available from the Library of Congress.

Contents

Introducing Wildflowers

Welcome! This book, along with its companion volume, *Eastern Washington and Oregon in Bloom*, is designed to introduce you to some of the most common and showy native wildflowers in our region. Western Washington and Oregon have more in common with one another than they do with the east side of the two states. We split the plants covered in this pair of books at the Cascade crest, the dividing line between the wetter west side and the dryer east side of each state. The chapter on climate, geography, and habitat goes into more detail.

In this book we set out to include 150 species that are both representative of the region's larger flora and likely to be seen in accessible natural areas. We put a lot of time and thought into selecting the plants you'll find here, but considering that this number is only a small fraction of the thousands of native and nonnative wildflowers, trees, shrubs, and grasses that grow in our region, it's quite likely we had to leave out many of the flowers you'll encounter while you're hiking, camping, or otherwise exploring.

While most trees, shrubs, and grasses also produce flowers, this book focuses on what are commonly called wildflowers or forbs—species lacking woody tissue that have showy flowers. To determine which wildflowers to include, we used our personal knowledge gained from exploring the Northwest and its plants for more than thirty years. We also consulted herbarium records and iNaturalist reports. The final result is a worthy selection of the diverse native wildflowers of western Washington and Oregon.

Getting to Know a Plant

It's easiest to identify plants when you adopt a systematic way of looking. While we're usually attracted first to the flowers and their shape and color, the rest of the plant is also important.

Start by getting an overall impression of the plant. Is it woody, like a tree or shrub? How big is it? Does it grow like a vine, form a mat on the ground, make a clump of stems, or have a single stem that stands by itself? Are the stems stiff and strong or are they flexible and slender? Are there any spines, prickles, or hairs?

Examine the leaves. Are they mostly right at the ground (basal) or do they grow along the stem? Some plants have both basal and stem leaves. What shape are the leaves? Leaf shapes are pictured inside the back cover. Stem leaves can be opposite each other or arranged alternately. Leaves can be attached to the stem with a stalk (called a petiole), clasp the stem, have little appendages at the attachment point (stipules), or appear to have the stem growing through the leaf. Many plants have compound leaves with several leaflets. You may need to count the leaflets and note how they're arranged. Leaf texture is another clue. Are they soft, leathery, hairy on one or both sides, or spiny?

Study the flowers. Identification usually requires a close look at the color, arrangement, and number of the flowering parts. Color is obvious, but it may change as the flowers age or among individuals of the same species. Sometimes petals have spots or blotches of a second color. Count the petals, if there are any. Some flowers don't have any petals, or they are very small and inconspicuous. Count the sepals, located at the base of the flower. For many plants, this will be enough to make an identification. However, you may also need to look closely to see how many stamens there are. Sometimes you need to see whether these sex parts are longer or shorter than the petals. For a few flowers, such as penstemons, you have to look closely to see how thick the hairs are inside and outside the flower. A 10× hand lens is useful for this close level of examination, can add a lot to your enjoyment of wildflowers, and doesn't weigh much in your pack. The visual glossary inside the front and back covers and the more extensive glossary beginning on page 377 can help you with technical terms you haven't yet learned.

Observe the habitat. Does the plant grow in the forest or out in the open? What is the soil like? What else is growing around your plant? Are you at the seashore, in the mountains, or somewhere in between? All of these are clues you can use to help you learn new plants.

Organization

Flowers in this book are arranged first by flower color, then by family, genus, and species. This keeps related flowers of the same color together while helping introduce the important botanical concepts of how plants are related to each other but also unique in some way.

The fastest way to look up an unknown flower is to turn to the appropriate color section and then leaf through the pages until you find one that looks a lot like the plant in front of you. Then study the photographs closely and read the descriptions until you find a match. Use the maps to eliminate plants that don't grow where you are. You may find it helpful to read the descriptions a second time, perhaps with a friend who looks closely at the plant while you read. We couldn't avoid using some technical terms and it may take you some time to learn their meanings. The alternative was circumlocution, using many words to convey the meaning of a short, precise, but more technical word.

Because flower color can vary, you may not find a plant in the section where you expect it. Creamy whites are included with the white flowers, but pale yellows are with the darker yellows. Sometimes the distinction isn't very clear. Reddish purple flowers are with the reds, but bluish purples are with the blues. Keep in mind that flower colors often vary within a species or change after pollination. For example, western trillium's open, brilliant white blossoms fade to pink and eventually to a deep red after they've been pollinated. You'll find it in the white section, not with the reds. Harsh paintbrush can have red, orange, or yellow flowers, with flowers of different colors often growing in the same area. It has been put in the pink and red section here. Both of these examples show the value of looking at the whole plant and, if available, several plants of the same species when trying to identify it.

The index includes the common and Latin names for the plants described in the book. If you know a plant's name but aren't sure what it looks like, then turn to the index to find it quickly.

Plant Names

Each plant species has a unique Latin name, which has two parts: the genus and the specific epithet. For a few plants, subspecies and varieties are listed, but for the most part this book sticks to identifying plants at the species level. Because plant names can change over time, generally due to additional DNA-based botanical research, we've listed Latin synonyms for some plants. The first name listed is the accepted name at the time of publication. We follow the Washington Flora Checklist and the Oregon Flora Checklist. If they disagree, we evaluate the reasons why the names are different and use the one that we judge to be preferable for our purposes. The alternate names are usually older names that have been superseded but are still in common use or found in technical volumes that haven't been updated recently.

Each plant also has one or more common names. The same plant may be called by different names in different places, or the same name may refer to different plants in different places. Some plants have so many common names we couldn't list them all.

Photographs

In most cases there is one photograph for each plant. They were selected to show as many of the important identifying characteristics as possible. Flowers receive more emphasis than foliage, which may appear somewhat soft-focus or in the background. Use the photographs to get a general feel for what the plant looks like, then read the description. Unfortunately, it is often impossible to show all pertinent characteristics in a single photograph.

Maps

Each plant in this book has a map that shows the counties with records of the plant having been found there. The maps, which include adjacent areas in British Columbia and California, are based on plant collections housed at herbariums in the Northwest, along with records from iNaturalist. Herbaria contain collections of dried, pressed plants that have been identified and annotated by professional botanists. They are mostly housed at universities, although some national parks and other organizations have their own herbaria. iNaturalist collects observations from community scientists, with many of the observations confirmed by professionals. While we think the maps are pretty accurate as of publication, they should be used as a guide only, as you might find a plant in a county with no records of its occurrence, especially if it's been found in the surrounding counties.

Descriptions

Each plant entry has several sections:

Habitat: We use a few words to describe where the plant most commonly grows. If you're in a low-elevation environment and the description says the plant grows in mid-montane to alpine locations you probably need to look a little farther to find the right match. The chapter on climate and habitat can help you interpret the information in this section.

Bloom: Most of our wildflowers bloom in spring or summer, with only a handful blooming in fall or late winter. The bloom seasons listed generally correspond to calendar seasons, but spring conditions can begin as early as February in warmer parts of our region. Some of our alpine plants bloom as soon as the snow melts, but that may not be until July, so they're listed as summer bloomers.

Description: This section gives an overall picture of the plant, including its height and whether it's an annual, biennial, or perennial.

Flowers: Flowers are generally described from the bottom up, which mostly means first describing bracts below the flower (if any), then sepals, and finally the petals (if any) and sex parts. Sometimes what looks like a petal is actually a sepal; we use "tepal" when these parts can't be easily classified as either sepals or petals.

Leaves: Leaves are described from the base of the plant and then up the stem. When the leaves grow at the base of the plant, they're basal. Stem leaves can be arranged alternately on the stem, opposite each other, or in a circlelike whorl. Leaves can be either simple or compound, the latter meaning they're divided into multiple leaflets that can sometimes be confused with individual leaves.

Fruit: Seeds are located within the fruit, but often they don't resemble the fleshy fruit you find at the grocery store. For example, many plants have a dry, one-seeded fruit that never opens to release the seed inside, called an achene. Sometimes the achene will have a feathery attachment (like dandelion fluff).

Descriptive text: This section for each plant gives some interesting additional information such as how to distinguish from look-alike species.

Exploring for
Wildflowers

Nearly everywhere you go, even in the concrete jungle in the middle of big cities like Seattle, Portland, or Spokane, you'll find wildflowers (and likely nonnative weeds as well). In our region, with its winter-wet and summer-dry climate, most of our native flowers bloom in spring. As the flush of flowers wanes in the lowlands, the higher elevations burst into bloom with the snowmelt. There are a few species that bloom at lower elevations in summer, or bloom in fall, but they're the exceptions to the rule.

You'll find the highest concentration of wildflowers in open habitats such as meadows, the shrub-steppe, and along forest edges. Deep in the shade of our forests not enough sunlight reaches the ground for many flowers to grow and bloom, although a handful are adapted to this shady environment. Roadsides and the borders of hiking trails are often quite floriferous, sometimes with large populations of the same species. Flowers are generally picky about the conditions where they thrive, so you won't find all the plants in this book everywhere you go. The chapter on climate and habitat gives more information on plant environments.

Access, Fees, and Permits

Wildflowers don't respect property boundaries; they grow wherever the conditions are right, regardless of whether their roots are sunk into public or private land. Many landowners are justifiably concerned about strangers wandering across their property, even if it's just to look at the flowers.

Ask permission before going onto private land. Remember to leave gates the way you found them and to walk softly.

Public lands are generally open to wildflower explorers, but entrance or parking fees may be required. These charges can change from year to year and are not consistent from one state to another nor on public lands managed by different agencies. Before venturing out, it's worth checking with the relevant land-management agency to find out whether you'll be charged. The fees help maintain the parking areas and may also help with trail construction.

Private preserves, such as those owned by The Nature Conservancy or local conservation groups, also vary in their access restrictions. Usually there is no fee, but donations are gratefully accepted.

Learning About Flowers

This book is an introduction to the wildflowers in our region. We kept the technical jargon to a minimum, but especially if you're new to botany you're sure to encounter some words you don't know. We used them because they more clearly describe the plants without getting overly wordy with convoluted circumlocutions. Over time, these terms will become more familiar. For now, use the glossary and the illustrations on the inside covers to get up to speed on the language.

We've placed the scientific name first with each plant description. While professional plant taxonomists have been busy updating our knowledge about how plants are related through DNA research and changing many scientific names in recent decades, there's still just one accepted scientific name for each species. That's not the case for common names. Some plants have multiple common names, and some refer to more than one species, which can lead to confusion.

Other Books and Apps

As your interest grows, you may want to further your knowledge with books that include more species. *Wildflowers of the Pacific Northwest* by Turner and Gustafson covers 1220 species and *Trees and Shrubs of the Pacific Northwest* by Turner and Kuhlmann includes 568 woody plants. Many people now look to plant apps for their smartphone. *Washington Wildflowers* and *Oregon Wildflowers*, both from High Country Apps, are comprehensive references for those states and were developed in cooperation with the plant professionals at the University of Washington and Oregon State University, respectively. They're not "point your camera at a plant and get an ID" apps but they include easy-to-use search tools. As your knowledge grows, you may ultimately decide one or more technical references are worth the investment.

Serious botanists rely on technical, dichotomous keys to definitively identify the plants they find. These books can be intimidating, but they go into much greater detail than is possible in a book like this one and allow for more definitive separation between similar species. Technical floras are heavy on specialized terminology and may call for you to use a hand lens to examine the flower parts or other small features to see distinguishing characteristics. Visit your library or a nearby herbarium to look up plants in these books before you invest in a copy.

There are three published floras for the region. Washington and Oregon as far south as Roseburg are covered in *Flora of the Pacific Northwest* by Hitchcock and Cronquist, which is updated and abbreviated from the five-volume *Vascular Plants of the Pacific Northwest*. The three-volume *Flora of Oregon* covers that state. Southern Oregon flora is more related to Northern California, so you might want to consult *The Jepson Manual: Vascular Plants of California*.

The "Going Further" chapter lists additional books you might want to consider as you expand your plant knowledge.

Websites

Many websites have a wealth of information about native plants. In Washington, the Burke Herbarium Image Collection is a highly regarded reference. In Oregon, it's OregonFlora. USDA PLANTS covers the entire United States and has good distribution information. iNaturalist, available both on the web and as a smartphone app, is another good online tool. The Washington Native Plant Society website (wnps.org) has numerous plant descriptions and lists of plants found along many trails in the state. These lists can help you narrow down the choices when trying to determine what plant you've found.

You can also use your favorite search engine and enter the Latin name of the plant you want to learn more about as the search term. Like all web searches, there will be some irrelevant results, so you'll need to evaluate the source before deciding how reliable it is likely to be.

Field-trip participants gather around leader Abe Lloyd as he shows the difference between native and nonnative cranberries in a bog near Bellingham, Washington.

Like-Minded Flower Explorers

It's more fun to go looking for flowers with other people who share your interest. There are native plant societies in both Washington and Oregon. Local chapters sponsor field trips to prime wildflower locations throughout the season and welcome nonmembers who want to learn more about their flora. You'll find announcements of these field trips on the organization's website. Search "native plant society" to find them.

Some other groups that lead plant hikes and field trips include parks and recreation departments, Sierra Club, The Mountaineers, and Audubon Society groups. Check the organization's website for information.

Die by the Foot, Grow by the Inch

Sometimes we get so carried away with the excitement of finding new and interesting plants that we forget to pay attention to the impact we're making on their environment. You've heard the adage, "Take nothing but pictures and leave nothing but footprints." But often even our lightest footprints do significant damage. National Park rangers like to remind us that plants "die by the foot and grow by the inch." Our footsteps easily break delicate woody stems that take years to grow back, particularly in subalpine and alpine environments with short growing seasons. They compact the soil, reducing the air and water reaching roots, and they form social paths that other hikers follow.

A simple sign reminds hikers to stay on the trail.

You can minimize your impact by following Leave No Trace (LNT) principles. They're designed to protect wild lands, but LNT principles apply equally well in heavily traveled areas. They are (1) Plan ahead and prepare, (2) Travel and camp on durable surfaces, (3) Dispose of waste properly (pack it in, pack it out), (4) Leave what you find, (5) Minimize campfire impacts, (6) Respect wildlife, and (7) Be considerate of other visitors. Much information on LNT techniques is available at lnt.org.

Perhaps most important for the wildflower hunter is to travel on durable surfaces. You don't want to be responsible for destroying the very plants you've come to find and enjoy. If there is an established trail, stay on it. In some cases, as in heavily visited national parks, you absolutely must stay on established trails and rangers will remind you of the policy when they find you have strayed. You'll often find more examples of a plant that's a bit too far off the trail to examine just by hiking a little farther on.

In areas where there are no trails, you don't want to create a "user trail" that will encourage others to follow in your footsteps. Think about where you're walking and consider the consequences of your actions. Perhaps you can step from rock to rock. If not, grasses and sedges handle footsteps better than woody plants like heathers and huckleberries. When hiking with a group, practice "meadow walking." That means to spread out and hike side by side rather than follow the leader in a single-file line.

When you come to an interesting plant that you want to study, be aware of what you're trampling as you move around your subject. Be careful where you set your pack down. And when it's time for lunch, choose a rock, log, or grassy area to sit down.

With rare exceptions, you don't need to pick a flower to identify it. Leave the plant collecting to the professionals who have learned the techniques for preserving specimens and have received permission to collect from land managers.

Safety

Searching for wildflowers is generally a low-risk activity, but there are hazards you should be aware of.

Rainy days can be a great time to explore for wildflowers, but dress for the weather like these participants on a Washington Native Plant Society field trip.

Weather

What starts as a beautiful warm and sunny day can quickly turn cold, windy, and rainy, particularly in mountain environments. Dress appropriately for the conditions and be prepared for unexpected changes.

Poisonous Plants

In some areas poison oak is thick. Learn to recognize its distinctive three leaves and woody stems. Some people are particularly sensitive to the rash-inducing chemicals in the leaves and stems. Poison ivy is similar, but much less common in our region. Stinging nettles are another irritant to watch out for, although the effects don't last as

Poison oak (*Toxicodendron diversilobum*) in autumn with its characteristic three leaflets and white berries. All parts of the plant can cause an unpleasant skin reaction.

long. Poison hemlock (page 63) is a common nonnative weed that is a significant skin irritant and deadly poisonous if eaten, even in small quantities.

Rattlesnakes

Watch where you step and where you place your hands. Though more prevalent east of the Cascades, rattlesnakes are also found in the Columbia Gorge and in oak woodlands in the Klamath/Siskiyou Mountains and Rogue River, Umpqua, and Willamette valleys. They'll usually sound their distinctive warning rattle before you get too close, but you don't want to surprise or corner one. They're not particularly common and you're unlikely to see one of these generally shy reptiles but be cautious when you're in their territory.

Ticks

Ticks are common in parts of our region, especially in tall grasses and weeds. They usually take several hours to attach themselves, so you have time to do a thorough tick check when you return to your car or home.

Traffic

Many wildflowers grow at the side of roads, whether they're main highways or forest roads. Find a safe place to pull over and park, making sure you're out of the travel lane. Walk on the left, facing traffic. Stay well out of the road when examining the flowers. Even on lightly traveled forest roads you should expect vehicles to come by while you're stopped.

Rockfall

You don't want to be either the cause or the victim of falling rock. Many areas with interesting flowers are on or near cliffs. Volcanic rock, our most common geologic formation, is often fractured and loose. Even on trails, it's easy to kick rocks down on people hiking the switchbacks below. If you do dislodge a rock, be sure to yell out "rock!" to alert anyone below.

Rising Tide

There aren't many wildflowers right on the beach, but several species do like to grow just above the high-tide line or on top of coastal sea stacks. If you climb one, make sure you don't get trapped by a rising tide. Consult a tide table just as you would before exploring the tide pools that are often nearby.

Your Own Limits

Know your limits—how far you can hike in a day and how much elevation you can climb (and descend). As you approach or exceed your limits, you're more likely to have an accident.

Have Fun

Searching for and learning about our wildflowers is a lot of fun, whether you're a certified Hitchcock-carrying plant nut or a beginner. There's always a new plant to find or a new place to go. You can casually enjoy and learn about them as you go backpacking, kayaking, visiting historic sites, or go out intentionally searching for plants. There are enough flowers in the Northwest to keep you busy for years if you choose to try to find them all. Explore the trails through your neighborhood or travel to an exotic corner of the state. The choice is yours. But wherever you go, you're likely to find something in bloom if the season is right.

Glacier lilies (*Erythronium grandiflorum*), generate heat as they grow, melting the last vestiges of snow as they emerge and bloom.

Climate, Geography, and Plant Habitats

Washington and Oregon share similarities in climate, geography, and plant habitats. In broad terms, west of the Cascade crest gets the majority of its precipitation in winter, followed by dry but relatively cool summers. East of the mountains, precipitation still comes mainly in the winter months, but there's not as much of it and summers are considerably hotter. Both states have mountain ranges near the Pacific coast, a broad interior valley, the north-south Cascade Range, a wide relatively flat expanse east of the Cascades, and slopes that rise to the Rocky Mountains along their eastern borders.

However, we also have many localized microclimates and habitats that have major impacts on our flora. For example, Forks, on the Olympic coast in Washington, gets a whopping 116 inches of rain each year. In the Olympic rain shadow, Ebey's Landing on Whidbey Island receives only about 20 inches of rain. Mount Vernon, less than 40 miles to the northeast, averages 37 inches annually. Going another 50 miles east, Marblemount averages 83 inches of rain each year. East of the Cascades, Yakima and the Tri-Cities only get about 8 inches, but rainfall slowly increases as you head east to Spokane, which averages about 16 inches annually. Oregon has similar changes as one moves from the coast inland. Seaside gets 75 inches, Salem averages 38 inches, Bend gets about 12 inches, and Halfway, on the Idaho border, averages about 20 inches.

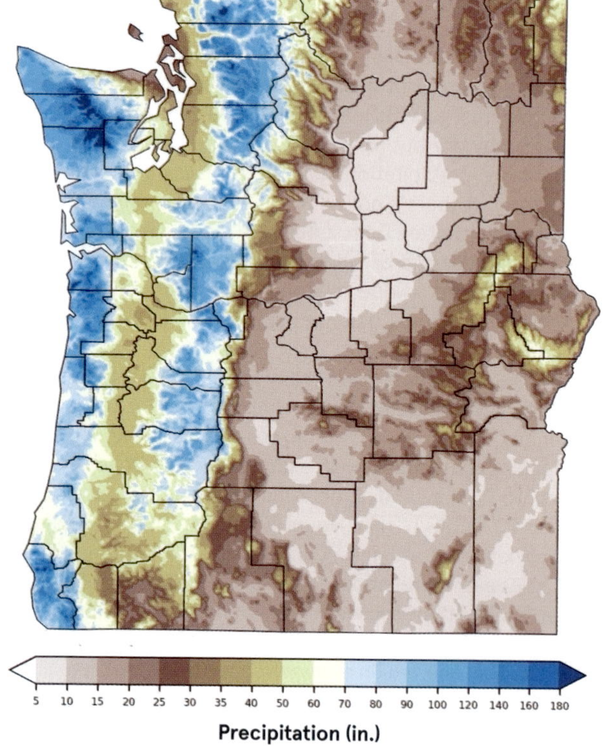

1981–2010 average annual precipitation for Washington and Oregon, mapped by the Western Regional Climate Center using data from the PRISM Climate Group at Oregon State University. Source maps available online at wrcc.dri.edu/Climate/prism_precip_maps.php.

Our weather predominately originates over the Pacific Ocean and is strongly influenced by both the Coast and Cascade mountain ranges as it moves eastward. As rain clouds get pushed up against the mountains, they lose most of their moisture, leading to the dense green forests and fields on the west side and the dry sagebrush-steppe habitat common to the east. As the air moves farther east, it starts picking up moisture again, only to lose it again on the western slopes of the Rocky Mountains.

Most of our precipitation, on both sides of the mountains, comes in winter and in many areas much of it arrives as snow. When the jet stream swings north in summer, we experience weeks with little rain. Our weather, at least in the western lowlands where most of us live, is generally mild thanks to the moderating influence of the Pacific Ocean. Of course, east of the Cascades the oceanic influence is less and therefore the temperatures are more extreme. We also experience a north-south temperature gradient, with warmer summers in southern Oregon than northern Washington.

Elevation is also an important factor in plant habitats, affecting both temperature and precipitation. At higher elevations in the Olympics and the Cascades, deep winter snow usually lingers until mid-July. Mountain snowfall melts a bit earlier in the Klamath Mountains in southern Oregon and in the Wallowa Mountains, which don't get as much snow as the Cascades. The North Cascades have the largest number of glaciers in the lower 48 states, a long-term result of the heavy snowfall they experience most winters. However, as the earth has warmed over the past decades many of these glaciers are slowly disappearing, leaving U-shaped valleys in their wake.

With higher temperatures and less precipitation, the broad expanse of the Columbia Plateau can't support trees except in sheltered draws and riparian zones adjacent to waterways. Instead, sagebrush and other shrub communities predominate. In contrast, with mild winters and copious rainfall, western Washington and Oregon have extensive conifer forests with some of the world's largest trees.

Washington and Oregon have complex geology, which determines the soils derived from the underlying rocks. While large areas of both states are underlain by basalt and other volcanic rocks, there are also areas with sedimentary rocks like sandstone and limestone. And in a few areas, ultramafic rocks have been lifted from deep within the earth's crust to the surface. These ultramafic rocks are commonly called serpentine. You'll find serpentine primarily in the Klamath-Siskiyou Mountains in Oregon and in the Wenatchee Mountains in Washington. We also have areas of granite as our bedrock. All of these base rocks erode to different types of soil, and these soils influence which plants grow there. Serpentine-derived soils are infertile, with low levels of key minerals such as phosphorus and calcium and relatively high levels of magnesium, chromium, and nickel. Areas with serpentine soils often have a relatively large number of endemic plants that are able to tolerate or thrive in places that inhibit the growth of many species.

Soil depth is another factor influencing plant growth. Thin soils on rocky ridges support plants that have adapted to these conditions. Where soils are deeper and there's more moisture, faster-growing species crowd out the slow-growing ones. It's not so much that the plants that live in harsh conditions can't grow in better conditions as that they are often outcompeted. Challenging environments are often home to a greater diversity of plant species, while the resource-rich habitats tend toward more uniform and homogenous plant communities.

As a result of our summer-dry climate, most of our wildflowers bloom in spring and early summer both east and west of the Cascades. High in the mountains, many flowers emerge and bloom immediately after the snow melts. A few, like glacier and avalanche lilies, even generate enough heat from their bulbs to melt the last bit of snow and may bloom still surrounded by the white stuff. Wetland plants that are not water-limited often bloom in mid- to late summer.

Ecoregions

Ecoregions, which are a way to group areas considering the relationships of precipitation, geology, physiography, vegetation, climate, soils, land use, wildlife, and hydrology, are a convenient way to understand the ecology of an area at a high level. Mapping all of North America from Alaska to Mexico, there are three levels of ecoregions, with increasing levels of detail from the big-picture Level I to the more detailed Level III. In the conterminous United States, mapping has been extended to an even more detailed Level IV. The concept was first developed in the late 1970s for the US Forest Service. For our purposes, we'll be using the Level III ecoregions defined by the US Environmental Protection Agency in cooperation with agencies in Canada and Mexico (epa.gov/eco-research/ecoregions-north-america).

Within each ecoregion you can expect to find broadly similar growing conditions and thus a more predictable pattern of plant communities and plant types. Of course, hyperlocal conditions also play a big role. Examples include environmental factors such as aspect—whether you're on the north or south slope of a mountain; light—the full sun of a meadow or deep in the shade of a forest; and elevation—a valley bottom versus along a ridgetop.

Ecoregions of Washington and Oregon

Washington and Oregon include all or parts of twelve ecoregions. We describe them here from north to south and west to east.

Coast Range

The Coast Range includes most of the Olympic Peninsula in Washington (except the high mountains at the core of Olympic National Park) and continues down the west side of Oregon and into the northwest corner of California. It has a maritime climate with warm, mostly dry summers and mild, very wet winters. Averaging 84 inches of annual precipitation, some areas get as much as 200 inches. All that rain

Old-growth western hemlocks (*Tsuga heterophylla*) along the Enchanted Valley Trail in Olympic National Park.

helps support dense coniferous forests, with Sitka spruce dominating along the coast and a mosaic of Douglas-fir, western hemlock, and western red cedar farther inland. Coast redwood is found in the far south of Oregon and in California. Much of the area has been heavily logged and replanted in Douglas-fir plantations. Larger communities in this ecoregion include Forks and Aberdeen, Washington; Astoria, Seaside, Tillamook, Newport, and Coos Bay, Oregon; and Crescent City and Eureka, California.

Puget Lowland

The Puget Lowland ecoregion incorporates eastern Vancouver Island and the Strait of Georgia lowlands in British Columbia, the lowlands around Puget Sound, and an area extending south to beyond Kelso, Washington. The climate is mild, with warm, dry summers and cool wet winters with

Profusion of spring wildflowers, including common camas (*Camassia quamash*), buttercups (*Ranunculus* spp.), field chickweed (*Cerastium arvense*), and harsh paintbrush (*Castilleja hispida*), on Yellow Island in Washington's San Juan Islands. Protected from development, Yellow Island is a Nature Conservancy preserve with limited public access.

occasional snow that usually melts quickly. There's a wide variation in annual rainfall, ranging from 12 inches in the Olympic rain shadow to 98 inches at higher elevations. While there are some low mountains, including the Chuckanuts south of Bellingham, most of the area is relatively flat to hilly. Relatively little undisturbed land remains in this highly urbanized region. Forests are dominated by Douglas-fir, western hemlock, grand fir, western red cedar, red alder, bigleaf maple, and a dense understory of species like salal, sword fern, Oregon-grape, and moss. Drier coastal areas often have Garry oak, shore pine, and Pacific madrone. Major population centers are Vancouver, Victoria, and Nanaimo, British Columbia; and Bellingham, Mount Vernon, Everett, Seattle, Tacoma, Olympia, and Centralia, Washington.

Willamette Valley

The Willamette Valley lies between the Coast Range and the Cascades in Oregon. It's generally warmer than the similar Puget Lowland to the north, with warm and dry summers and mild, wet winters. Annual rainfall ranges from 35 to 63 inches, with the mountainous foothills on the east side of the valley getting the most. Once home to extensive native prairies, savannahs and forests, deciduous riparian forests, and seasonal wetlands, most of the Willamette Valley has been converted to agriculture. Natural areas feature Garry oak woodlands, prairies, and Douglas-fir or valley ponderosa pine woodlands. Riparian areas have black cottonwood, Oregon ash, bigleaf maple, alder, western red cedar, and a

Wet prairies like this one at Deer Creek Prairie Park near Sheridan, Oregon, were common before agriculture came to dominate the Willamette Valley. The purple flowers are common camas (*Camassia quamash*). This prairie had been converted to farmland and is undergoing restoration to preserve some rare plant species.

variety of shrubs. This gentle, rolling landscape is home to most of Oregon's population. Portland, Gresham, Beaverton, Hillsboro, Salem, Albany, Corvallis, Eugene, and Springfield are the major communities.

Klamath Mountains

The Klamath Mountains are rugged and highly dissected with steep slopes, located south of the Willamette Valley and between the Coast Range and the Cascades in southwestern Oregon and adjacent California. Although the Mediterranean climate is generally mild, summers in the valleys can be quite warm with lengthy periods of drought and relatively mild winters. The geology is complex and diverse, with sandstones and shales, granitic intrusive rocks, and substantial areas

Western azaleas (*Rhododendron occidentale*) and Jeffrey pines (*Pinus jeffreyi*) at the edge of a fen at the Eight Dollar Mountain Botanical Trail near Selma, Oregon. California pitcher plants (*Darlingtonia californica*) are nearly hidden among the grasses and sedges in the foreground.

with ultramafic rocks (serpentine) and the unique plant communities that grow there. Precipitation varies from 20 inches in the lower and dryer areas to 118 inches on the higher mountains, with much of that falling as winter snow. The Klamaths have the greatest conifer diversity of any place on the planet, but you'll also find tanoak, Garry oak, Pacific madrone, California black oak, chinkapin, and canyon live oaks here. Common conifers include Douglas-fir, white fir, incense cedar, Jeffrey pine, Shasta red fir, sugar pine, ponderosa pine, and western juniper. Larger communities include Roseburg, Grants Pass, Medford, and Ashland, Oregon; and Yreka and Weaverville, California.

North Cascades

The North Cascades include the northern end of the Cascade Range in northwest Washington and southern British Columbia, spanning both sides of the mountains between the Puget Lowland and the Columbia Plateau. This region also includes a disjunct area, the high Olympic Mountains at the core of Olympic National Park. Much of the area is national forest and national parklands. Climate here varies considerably, with temperate rainforest conditions at lower elevations in the west, a dry continental climate in the east, and deep winter snow and a short growing season in the high mountains in between. Summers are warm and dry; winters cool to cold and wet, with much of the precipitation coming as snow. The Mount Baker Ski Area set the record for the world's highest snowfall in one season during the winter of 1998–1999 with 1140 inches (95 feet) of snow. There are more glaciers here than in any other region of the United States outside of Alaska. Lower slopes on the west side are dominated by Douglas-fir, western hemlock, and western red cedar. Higher in the mountains you'll find Engelmann spruce,

Lewis's monkeyflowers (*Erythranthe lewisii*), cow parsnips (*Heracleum maximum*), and broadleaf lupines (*Lupinus latifolius*) fill a subalpine meadow along the Heliotrope Ridge Trail approaching Mount Baker.

silver fir, subalpine fir, whitebark pine, and mountain hemlock. Descending the slopes to the east, the forest transitions to Douglas-fir, ponderosa pine, and lodgepole pine. Larger communities include Concrete, Marblemount, Winthrop, Twisp, and Leavenworth, Washington.

Cascades

The Cascades stretch from west-central Washington south through the spine of Oregon, and include a disjunct area in Northern California. The Cascades of Washington and Oregon are home to many volcanoes including Mount Rainier, Mount Adams, Mount Saint Helens, Mount Hood, Mount Jefferson, the Three Sisters, and Crater Lake, a caldera formed from the collapse of Mount Mazama. Large portions of this ecoregion are public lands. Summers are mostly dry and warm, with

Magenta paintbrush (*Castilleja parviflora* var. *oreopola*), broadleaf lupine (*Lupinus latifolius*), and numerous other species of wildflowers grow along a small stream in Cispus Basin in the Goat Rocks Wilderness near Packwood, Washington.

relatively mild to cool, very wet winters. Annual precipitation varies from 45 to 142 inches, depending on elevation and latitude with much of the higher-elevation precipitation coming as snow. Highly productive coniferous forests blanket most of the region, with Douglas-fir, western hemlock, western red cedar, bigleaf maple, and red alder at lower elevations. Higher up, Pacific silver fir, mountain hemlock, subalpine fir, noble fir, and lodgepole pine dominate. In the southern part of the region, you'll find Shasta red fir and white fir. The highest elevations have extensive subalpine meadows and rocky alpine zones. Few people live in this region; larger communities include Stevenson, Washington, and Cascade Locks and Oakridge, Oregon.

Eastern Cascades Slopes and Foothills

The Eastern Cascades lie in the rain shadow of the Cascades region, running from central Washington to Northern California. The climate is more continental, with less precipitation and greater temperature extremes than in the mountains to the west. Summers are warm, bordering on hot, and dry, while winters are cold. Precipitation ranges from 20 to 138 inches, with the higher amount coming mostly as snow on the higher peaks. Historically, forests were somewhat open parkland with ponderosa and lodgepole pines, with shrub-steppe and grasslands dominating in the drier east. Vegetation is adapted to the dry continental climate, but is also highly susceptible to wildfire, especially after fire suppression over many decades led to a denser understory. The land has gently to steeply sloping mountains and high plateaus, interspersed with volcanic cones and some young lava flows. Like the Cascades and North Cascades, much of the land here is national forest or other public lands. Communities include Hood River, Bend, Klamath Falls, and Lakeview, Oregon.

Davidson's penstemon (*Penstemon davidsonii*) brightens a rocky outcrop on Black Butte near Bend, Oregon. Mount Jefferson is on the horizon.

Columbia Plateau

The Columbia Plateau covers a huge portion of central and southeastern Washington and a wide band of northern Oregon south of the Columbia River between The Dalles and Pendleton. Underlain by thick layers of basalt, this region has dry, mid-latitude desert and steppe climates with hot, dry summers and cold winters. Precipitation comes mostly in winter, ranging from 6 inches in the rain shadow on the western edge to 23 inches in the northeast part of the region. Few trees grow here, except in the riparian zones along the Columbia River and its tributaries. Sagebrush, bitterbrush, and rabbitbrush are the taller shrubs, growing among a sea of grasses that include bluebunch wheatgrass, needle and thread, Sandberg bluegrass, and Idaho fescue. Invasive and extremely flammable cheatgrass has overtaken much of the region. Columnar basalt cliffs separating tablelands from the river valleys are common here, while other areas are covered by thick loess deposits. Irrigated agriculture is common and in the rolling hills of the Palouse, dryland wheat and pulse

Big sagebrush *(Artemisia tridentata)* among the basalt cliffs on the Seep Lakes Wildlife Management Area between Moses Lake and Othello, Washington.

crops dominate. Larger population centers include Wenatchee, Ellensburg, Yakima, Richland, Kennewick, Pasco, Walla Walla, and Hermiston, Washington; and Pendleton and The Dalles, Oregon.

Northern Rockies

The Northern Rockies, the product of continental crust uplift, encompass the northeast corner of Washington, along with adjacent areas of British Columbia, northern Idaho, and

Shrubby penstemon (*Penstemon fruticosus*), sticky cinquefoil (*Drymocallis glandulosa*), and big sagebrush (*Artemisia tridentata*) on a rock outcrop along the Kettle Crest Trail on the Colville National Forest east of Republic, Washington.

northwestern Montana. Somewhat surprisingly, there's some maritime influence here so the forests include many of the same species as wetter areas to the west—Douglas-fir, western and mountain hemlocks, western red cedar, and grand fir, along with ponderosa and lodgepole pines, western white pine, subalpine fir, and Engelmann spruce. The climate is somewhat severe, with relatively dry, warm summers and cold, snowy winters with moisture increasing from south to north. Precipitation ranges from 16 to 79 inches, with the greatest amount falling on the highest mountains. Larger communities include Spokane, Colville, Republic, and Newport, Washington.

Blue Mountains

The Blue Mountains ecoregion covers much of northeastern Oregon and small portions of adjacent Washington and Idaho. Like the Cascades, but unlike the Northern Rockies, the Blue Mountains are mostly volcanic in origin, with only the high peaks of the Wallowa and Elkhorn mountains

A hiker passes Bonny Lake heading toward Aneroid Mountain in the Eagle Cap Wilderness.

consisting of intrusive rocks rising above the lava. The Blues are mostly lower and more open than other mountain ranges in the Northwest. The climate has both continental and Mediterranean influences, with warm, dry summers and cold winters. Precipitation ranges from 9 inches in the low valleys to 80 inches at high elevations, with much of that coming as winter snow. Low elevations contain mostly grasslands with bluebunch wheatgrass and Idaho fescue, sagebrush-steppe, and juniper woodlands. Forested areas have Douglas-fir, ponderosa pine, and grand fir at lower elevations; and subalpine fir, Engelmann spruce, whitebark and lodgepole pine up high, along with alpine meadows. Population centers include Madras, Redmond, Prineville, La Grande, Baker City, and Enterprise, Oregon.

Snake River Plain

The Snake River Plain consists of plains and low hills centered on the Snake River that is incised into volcanic rocks.

Northern mule's ears (*Wyethia amplexicaulis*) in a meadow on the Pine Valley Ranch in Baker County, Oregon, with the Granite Mountains on the horizon.

Primarily in southern Idaho, a small part of this region extends into eastern Oregon between the Blue Mountains to the north and the Northern Basin and Range to the south. It is relatively flat with warm, dry summers and cold winters. Rainfall is sparse, ranging from 4 to 25 inches. Similar to the Columbia Plateau, this region has a sagebrush-steppe environment with sagebrush, bluebunch wheatgrass, Idaho fescue, Indian ricegrass, rabbitbrush, and fourwing saltbush as dominant species. Irrigation water is abundant, so many of the alluvial valleys near the Snake River are agricultural. Most of the population centers are in Idaho: Boise, Nampa, Pocatello, Idaho Falls, and Twin Falls, as well as Ontario, Oregon.

Northern Basin and Range

The Northern Basin and Range ecoregion covers the southeast quarter of Oregon and adjacent areas of northern Nevada and southern Idaho. It is drier than the Columbia Plateau and generally higher in elevation, making it less suitable for agriculture. It's arid, with mid-latitude steppe and desert climates, characterized by hot summers and cold winters. Precipitation ranges from 6 inches at lower elevations to more than 39 inches on the upper reaches of Steens Mountain. Geologically mixed, the region has tablelands, dissected lava plains, scattered north-south trending mountains, and valleys with gently sloping alluvial fans. Several lakes and wetlands are stopover points for migrating waterfowl. Basins are dominated by sagebrush-steppe habitat with several species of sagebrush, rabbitbrush, scattered junipers, bluebunch wheatgrass, Idaho fescue, and Thurber's needlegrass. Ranges have mountain sagebrush, mountain-mahogany, juniper, and Idaho fescue at lower to mid-elevations, with Douglas-fir and aspen common higher up. Few people live here, with Burns, Oregon, the largest community. Christmas Valley, Jordan Valley, Frenchglen, and Burns Junction are much smaller populated places.

Sagebrush phlox (*Phlox aculeata*) growing up through sagebrush in the vicinity of Jordan Valley, Oregon.

Habitats and Local Environments

Ecoregions describe broad areas with similar conditions, but if you've done any wandering about you've likely noticed that local environments play an important role in determining which plants grow there. For example, in the North Cascades ecoregion you'll find dense, relatively low-elevation forests, wetlands and other riparian zones, rocky balds, subalpine forests, and treeless alpine meadows. West- and south-facing slopes often support different plants than east- and north-facing ones. Within the Columbia Plateau, areas with thin and rocky soils support a surprisingly large assortment of plants, but they're not the same ones you'll find in places with a thicker soil layer.

The Pacific Northwest is generally a winter-wet, summer-dry environment. That means that most of our flowering plants put on their show in spring and early summer, before the soil dries out. In the mountains, places where snow lingers longer will have later-blooming flowers, often of the same species that might bloom earlier just a short distance away. The timing of the snowmelt is more important than calendar dates when looking for blooming wildflowers there.

Our coniferous forests have few wildflowers if the stand of trees is dense because not enough light reaches the forest floor. But within these dense forests are gaps that get more light—places where trees have fallen and opened the canopy, roadsides, edges of trails, and naturally occurring meadows. And some coniferous forests are more light-filled due to a lower tree density such as those on the eastern slopes of the Cascades that consequently have an abundance of spring wildflowers. Deciduous lowland forests, with their canopy of bigleaf maple, red alder, and black cottonwood, can have a profusion of early-season wildflowers that begin blooming before the trees have leafed out completely.

For each of the plants in this field guide we've used a few words to paint a picture of the habitats where you're most likely to find them. The habitat descriptions that follow cover both sides of the Cascades, even though this book focuses on just one side of the mountains. We hope that gives you a bigger picture of the habitat diversity here in the Northwest and might encourage you to explore the "other side of the mountains" if you haven't already.

Forests

The mix of trees in Northwest forests, and the wildflowers at their feet, depends on the soil in which they sink their roots, the availability of water, and elevation, which can be seen as a proxy for temperature. Coastal and west-slope forests are much wetter than those dominated by the ponderosa

Vanillaleaf (*Achlys triphylla*), lady ferns (*Athyrium filix-femina*), and sword ferns (*Polystichum munitum*) in the understory beneath old-growth Douglas-firs (*Pseudotsuga menziesii*) in the low-elevation westside forest at Rockport State Park, Washington.

Arrowleaf balsamroot (*Balsamorhiza sagittata*) and biscuitroots (*Lomatium* spp.) bloom under ponderosa pines (*Pinus ponderosa*) in an open eastside forest on the Okanogan-Wenatchee National Forest near Cashmere, Washington.

and lodgepole pines found east of the Cascades. Lowland forests are found below about 1500 feet. Montane forests grow on the slopes of our mountains from roughly 1500 to 4000 feet, with lower montane forests often carpeted with a dense layer of mosses dotted with wildflowers in the more open places. Above 4000 feet the forest thins, becoming subalpine up to the treeline, above which is the treeless alpine zone. You'll find forests in most of our ecoregions, with the exceptions of the Columbia Plateau and Northern Basin and Range which are too dry to support trees except adjacent to streams.

Alpine and Subalpine

Alpine and subalpine habitats are similar, the big difference being that true alpine areas are devoid of trees. In the subalpine, you'll find gradually thinning forests as you go higher, with pockets of trees dotting meadows and rocky slopes until you reach treeline. These are harsh environments,

Mountain arnica (*Arnica latifolia*) and broadleaf lupines (*Lupinus latifolia*) in an alpine meadow along the Ptarmigan Ridge trail approaching Mt. Baker.

with deep snow that lingers into mid-summer and a short growing season. South-facing slopes are often covered with dense flower-filled meadows, particularly where snowmelt water seeps into thicker soils. North-facing slopes, which melt out later, are more likely to have thin and rocky soils. Most plants in both the alpine and subalpine are perennials as establishing new plants from seed is challenging with the short growing season. Look for plants to bloom in these high-elevation areas soon after the snow melts, although there are some, like the gentians, grass-of-Parnassus, and asters, that bloom later in summer.

Shrub-Steppe

The shrub-steppe habitat occurs in large areas of eastern Washington and Oregon. With little rainfall, the largest plants are shrubs like sagebrush, rabbitbrush, and bitterbrush. They're widely spaced, with native bunchgrasses (and non-native cheatgrass) and wildflowers between them. Within the

Rock buckwheat (*Eriogonum sphaerocephalum*) blooms among big sagebrush (*Artemisia tridentata*) and bitterbrush (*Purshia tridentata*) beneath the basalt cliffs of the Yakima River Canyon near the Umtanum Recreation Site in eastern Washington.

shrub-steppe are areas with deep loamy soils, sand dunes, and thin, rocky soil areas called lithosols. You'll also find basalt cliffs that have wildflowers growing in their cracks. In some areas there are vernal pools, places where winter rains accumulate and then slowly evaporate in spring, often with successive rings of wildflowers around their edges.

Meadows and Prairies

Meadows and prairies are similar, with meadows generally smaller and at higher elevations. Prairies cover larger areas and often are drier or have thinner soils. The terms are sometimes used interchangeably. They're dominated by grasses, but often have profuse displays of wildflowers in spring. Both meadows and prairies can be wet or dry. Wet prairies are less common than they were before European settlers arrived and began draining them as they converted these bottomlands with rich soils to productive farmland, especially in Oregon's Willamette Valley. Mesic prairies have moderate moisture, being neither exceptionally wet nor dry.

Common camas (*Camassia quamash*) and western buttercups (*Ranunculus occidentalis*) blanket the mounded prairie at Mima Mounds Natural Area Preserve in Thurston County, Washington.

Broadleaf lupines (*Lupinus latifolius*), Sitka valerian (*Valeriana sitchensis*), and mountain arnica (*Arnica latifolia*) dominate the steep subalpine meadow below Excelsior Pass in the Mount Baker Wilderness near Glacier, Washington.

Wetlands

Wetlands are areas where water covers the soil or is near the soil surface all or part of the year. These can be riparian, bordering streams, rivers, or lakeshores. They can also be isolated areas within forests, meadows, or prairies. Wetlands can be perennial like bogs, fens, and swamps. They can also be seasonal, wet in winter and spring but drying out after the rains stop in summer. By the time autumn rolls around, a seasonal wetland may look like it could be dry year-round.

Skunk cabbage (*Lysichiton americanus*) brightens a forest wetland on the outskirts of Bellingham, Washington.

Coastal

Coastal habitats occupy a narrow strip of land adjacent to and near marine shorelines. Few plants grow directly on either rocky or sandy beaches that get inundated by salt water as the tide comes and goes. But at the back of the beach, you may find an assortment of grasses, sand verbena, beach morning glory, and other deep-rooted plants that help stabilize the shore. Some coastal areas have extensive undulating sand dunes, often with freshwater wetlands between drier forested areas. Dunes are most common on the Oregon coast between Florence and Coos Bay. Bluffs and headlands rise sharply from the coast, hosting wind-swept forests or dense shrub thickets.

Harsh paintbrush (*Castilleja hispida*) blooms on a grassy slope below the Deception Pass Bridge south of Anacortes, Washington.

Rocky Areas

Rock underlies every habitat, with the type of rock determining the soil on top. In some places, there's just rock with very little exposed soil. These rocky areas include the basalt cliffs common in eastern Washington and Oregon, the lithosols interspersed in the shrub-steppe, as well as the talus and scree slopes found in the mountains as freezing and thawing gradually break them down. Alpine or subalpine rocky areas are very different from those of the Columbia Plateau, but what they have in common are plants that send their roots down through cracks to find nutrients and moisture while their aboveground parts are blasted by the sun and wind.

Lewis's monkeyflowers (*Erythranthe lewisii*) and red willowherb (*Chamaenerion latifolium*) bloom on a moist talus slope below Bearpaw Mountain on the Mount Baker–Snoqualmie National Forest near Glacier, Washington.

Desert yellow daisies (*Erigeron linearis*) grow at the base of basalt cliffs near Wanapum Dam, a few miles south of Vantage, Washington.

Disturbed Areas

Disturbed areas include all the places where humans have changed the original natural habitat, as well as sites burned by naturally initiated wildfires or erosion. Road cuts, roadsides, farmland, vacant lots, clearcuts, and the edges of trails are all disturbed habitats. These areas are often dense with a diversity of plants, both native and nonnative. Many of our weeds, not included in this book, are particularly common in disturbed habitats.

Fireweed (*Chamaenerion angustifolium*) is among the first wildflowers to return following a forest fire. It's blooming here among burned lodgepole pines (*Pinus contorta*) along the Remmel Creek Trail in the Pasayten Wilderness north of Winthrop, Washington.

Putting It Together

Many factors affect the mosaic of habitats across the Pacific Northwest. Rocks determine the soils above them, whether they're thick and loamy or thin and rocky. Rainfall and snow depth vary dramatically across the region. Elevation plays a big role, as do slope, aspect, and exposure to the sun. Ecoregions sketch a broad picture of the environment, while individual habitats paint a more detailed look. As you hike or drive backroads, you'll come to learn the plants in these individual habitats and discover that the same or similar habitat in other places is home to the same or similar group of plants. We're fortunate to live in a part of the continent with such diversity.

White Flowers

Apiaceae—parsley family

Angelica arguta

sharptooth angelica, Lyall's angelica, shining angelica

HABITAT Streambanks, wetlands, wet meadows, lakeshores, lowland to subalpine

BLOOMS Spring, summer

DESCRIPTION Herbaceous perennial, mostly nonhairy, taprooted, stems erect, inflorescence umbrella-shaped, rays of the umbel with a small flower cluster at the tips, plants 1½–6½ ft. tall

FLOWERS Saucer-shaped, tiny, petals white, stamens 5, styles 2

LEAVES Alternate, broadly triangular, 3–12 in. long, pinnately divided, leaflets lance-shaped, ¾–6½ in. long by ½–3 in. wide, edges toothed, sometimes irregularly lobed, tips pointed

FRUIT Dry, oval to roundish, to ¼ in. long, winged, splits into 2 parts, each with 1 seed

Sharptooth angelica grows from Alaska south to California and east to Montana. It is not found near salt water; similar plants growing near the coast may be sea-watch (*A. lucida*) or Henderson's angelica (*A. hendersonii*). Sharptooth angelica is nontoxic but can be confused with the poisonous western water-hemlock (*Cicuta douglasii*).

Apiaceae—parsley family
Conium maculatum

poison hemlock

HABITAT Roadsides, ditches, streambanks, meadows, lowland to mid-montane

BLOOMS Spring, summer

DESCRIPTION Toxic herbaceous biennial, nonnative, malodorous, taprooted, stems erect with purple blotches, leaves fernlike, inflorescence lacy, umbrella-like, with small flower clusters gathered into larger ones at the stem tip and leaf axils, plants 1½–10 ft. tall

FLOWERS Tiny, petals 5, white, spoon- to heart-shaped, tips notched, stamens 5, longer than the petals, styles 2

LEAVES Alternate, stalked, nonhairy, outline of the blade triangular, 6–12 in. long, divided 3–4 times, ultimate segments small, shiny green, tips pointed

FRUIT Dry, egg-shaped, ribs curved, 2-seeded

A decoction of poison hemlock, a highly poisonous invasive weed native to Europe, is thought to have been used to kill Socrates in ancient Greece. Native species western water-hemlock (*Cicuta douglasii*) is highly poisonous as well. Western water-hemlock has similar white umbrella-shaped flower clusters, but in contrast to poison hemlock, it is a perennial, has much larger, lance-shaped leaflets, and lacks purple stem blotches.

Apiaceae—parsley family
Glehnia leiocarpa

American glehnia, beach carrot, beach silvertop

HABITAT Sand dunes and beaches, maritime, coastal, lowlands

BLOOMS Spring, summer

DESCRIPTION Herbaceous perennial, taprooted, stems short or absent, often buried in sand, all leaves basal, leathery, inflorescence umbrella-like, rays of the umbel with small cluster of flowers at the tip, plants to 4 in. tall

FLOWERS Tiny, petals 5, white, stamens 5, styles 2

LEAVES Basal, stalked, spreading, 1½–7 in. long, divided 1 or 2 times into leaflets, leaflets oval- to egg-shaped, edges toothed, upper surface nonhairy, lower surface densely woolly-hairy

FRUIT Dry, oblong to roundish, ribbed, to ½ in. long, 2-seeded

Usually found in shifting sand, American glehnia's low stature and leathery leaves minimize loss of moisture from wind and temperature fluctuations. Fruit of American glehnia float and are dispersed in seawater.

Apiaceae—parsley family
Heracleum maximum (Heracleum lanatum)

common cow-parsnip

HABITAT Streambanks, wetlands, meadows, lowland to mid-montane

BLOOMS Spring, summer

DESCRIPTION Sturdy herbaceous perennial, aromatic, hairy, roots fibrous or taprooted, stem 1, hollow, leaves maplelike, inflorescence umbrella-shaped, rays of the umbel with a flower cluster at the tip, plants 3–10 ft. tall

FLOWERS Tiny, stalked, petals 5, white, stamens 5

LEAVES Alternate, stalked, lower stem leaves divided in 3, leaflets 4–12 in. long, central lobe maplelike, the other 2 smaller, lower surface hairy, edges lobed and toothed, tips pointed, upper stem leaves lobed, not divided

FRUIT Dry, heart- to egg-shaped, 2-seeded

The watery sap of common cow-parsnip can irritate the skin, but the stems are considered edible if prepared properly. However, avoid contact with the similar-looking nonnative giant hogweed (*H. mantegazzianum*) as sap from this plant can cause severe skin burns and eye irritation. Considerably larger than common cow-parsnip, stems of giant hogweed have reddish purple blotches and blisters, while common cow-parsnip does not.

Araliaceae—ginseng family
Oplopanax horridus

devil's club

HABITAT Wetlands, streambanks, seeps, moist forests, lowland to mid-montane

BLOOMS Spring, summer

DESCRIPTION Perennial shrub, deciduous, stems erect to leaning, densely spiny, spines yellowish, to ¼ in. long, leaves large, maplelike, inflorescence a branched, pyramidal cluster of small flowers at the stem tip, plants 3–10 ft. tall

FLOWERS Tiny, sepals 5, inconspicuous, petals 5, greenish white, stamens 5, longer than the petals

LEAVES Alternate, stalks spiny, blades maplelike with 7–9 lobes, 4–14 in. wide, surface prickly beneath, edges toothed, tips pointed

FRUIT Berry, roundish, red, seeds 2 or 3, inedible

Devil's club is slow growing and drought intolerant. Spines from any part of the plant can cause skin irritation. Its berries are not considered edible for humans, but are prized by wildlife, particularly by bears and squirrels. Devil's club, which Native Americans traditionally utilize for medicinal purposes, is also being studied by researchers for its pharmacological potential.

Asparagaceae—asparagus family
Maianthemum dilatatum

wild lily-of-the-valley, false lily-of-the-valley, May lily

HABITAT Mesic forests, streambanks, shady edge habitats, lowland to mid-montane

BLOOMS Spring

DESCRIPTION Herbaceous perennial, rhizomatous, patch-forming, stems 1–3 per node, erect, leaves usually 2 per stem, inflorescence a narrow, oblong cluster of tiny, stalked flowers, fragrant, plant 4–14 in. tall

FLOWERS Cross-like, tepals 4, white, stamens 4

LEAVES Basal and alternate along the stem, stalks long, blades heart-shaped, 2–4 in. long, dark glossy green, veins parallel, prominent, tips pointed

FRUIT Berry, round, red, seeds 1–4

Wild lily-of-the-valley grows well in shady garden settings, best used as a groundcover as it spreads easily. Berries are edible but bitter, and highly valued by wildlife.

Asparagaceae—asparagus family
Maianthemum racemosum

large false Solomon's seal, western Solomon's plume

HABITAT Forest openings, streambanks, wet meadows, lowland to mid-montane

BLOOMS Spring, summer

DESCRIPTION Herbaceous perennial, rhizomatous, patch-forming, stems erect, inflorescence a dense, branched cluster of tiny flowers at the stem tip, plants 1–3 ft. tall

FLOWERS Fragrant, small, stalked, tepals 6, oblong, creamy white, stamens 6, wider than tepals, pistil 1

LEAVES Alternate, stalkless, blades oval, 3–8 in. long, shiny green, veins parallel, prominent, tips pointed

FRUIT Berry, round, reddish to bright red

Berries are edible but not considered palatable. The name false Solomon's seal comes from its resemblance to the Eastern US and Eurasian genus *Polygonatum* (Solomon's seal). The term Solomon's seal refers to the Hebrew King Solomon's legendary signet ring, which had a pentagram design. The rhizomes of *Polygonatum* spp. have pentagram-shaped scars, as if stamped by King Solomon's ring. *M. racemosum* ssp. *amplexicaule* grows in our region, while ssp. *racemosum*, with arching stems and stalked leaves, grows in the Midwest and Eastern United States.

Asparagaceae—asparagus family
Maianthemum stellatum

starry Solomon's seal, star-flowered Solomon's seal

HABITAT Mesic to dry forests, meadows, rocky slopes, streambanks, lowland to subalpine

BLOOMS Spring, summer

DESCRIPTION Herbaceous perennial, rhizomatous, patch-forming, stems erect, leafy, inflorescence an unbranched, few-flowered cluster at the stem tip, plants 6–24 in. tall

FLOWERS Star-shaped, fragrant, tepals 6, creamy white, oblong to lance-shaped, to ¼ in. long, stamens 6

LEAVES Alternate, stalk absent, blades flat to folded, oval to lance-shaped, 1–6 in. long, shiny green, edges smooth, tips pointed

FRUIT Berry, round, dark blue to reddish black, seeds 1–6

Starry Solomon's seal is found throughout Canada and most of the United States, except for the southern states. It grows on both sides of the Cascades in Washington and Oregon. The leaves of starry Solomon's seal are narrower and often folded in drier habitats and wider and unfolded in wetter areas. It grows well in garden settings; plant it in rich, well-drained soils in partial shade. The berries are edible, considered somewhat bitter and tart.

Asteraceae—aster family

Achillea millefolium

common yarrow, milfoil

HABITAT Forest openings, fields, meadows, shrub-steppe, disturbed areas, lowland to alpine

BLOOMS Spring, summer, fall

DESCRIPTION Herbaceous perennial, aromatic, rhizomatous, stems erect, sparsely to densely hairy, leaves fernlike, inflorescence a branched, flat-topped cluster of heads at the stem tip, plants 1–2 ft. tall

FLOWERS Bracts of the head hairy, in overlapping shingled rows, both ray and disk flowers, rays white to pink, disk flowers creamy white

LEAVES Basal and alternate on the stem, sparsely to densely hairy, stalked except those of upper stem stalkless, blades 1–14 in. long, lance-shaped, pinnately divided, lobes linear, tips pointed

FRUIT Achene, nonhairy

Highly aromatic, common yarrow contains a number of volatile oils, tannins, and other compounds such as salicylic acid, the active ingredient in aspirin. It has a long history of use as a medicinal herb, made into poultices, salves, and teas. Yarrow grows well in garden settings but may spread aggressively if not contained. Circumboreal in distribution.

Asteraceae—aster family
Petasites frigidus

arctic sweet coltsfoot, western coltsfoot, alpine coltsfoot

HABITAT Meadows, swamps, seeps, streambanks, lowland to alpine

BLOOMS Spring, summer

DESCRIPTION Herbaceous perennial, rhizomatous, stems erect, stem leaves bractlike, stems and flowers usually emerge before the basal leaves, flowers in heads, clusters branched at the stem tips, plants 3–18 in. tall

FLOWERS Heads bell-shaped, mostly unisexual, female heads with ray flowers, rays white and short, the male heads have all disk flowers

LEAVES Basal leaves stalked, triangular to kidney-shaped, from 1–12 in. long, blades 5–8 lobed, lobes palmate or pinnate, lower surface mostly white woolly-hairy

FRUIT Achene, topped by a hair tuft

High-elevation plants, var. *frigidus*, usually have basal leaves with pinnate lobing, while lower-elevation plants, var. *palmatus*, have palmate lobing. The name arctic sweet coltsfoot refers to the northern distribution of the species, its sweet-smelling flowers, and the similarity between its leaf shape and that of a horse's hoof.

Berberidaceae—barberry family
Achlys triphylla

vanillaleaf, deer foot, sweet after death

HABITAT Mesic forests, preferably shady, lowland to montane

BLOOMS Spring, summer

DESCRIPTION Herbaceous perennial, rhizomatous, stem 1, erect, leafless, nonhairy, inflorescence a terminal spike, plants 7–15 in. tall

FLOWERS Not showy, sepals and petals absent, stamens 8–13, mostly 10, white, pistil 1, style absent

LEAVES Basal, blades 2–8 in. across, palmately divided into 3 leaflets, leaflets fan-shaped, edges lobed, lobe tips rounded, stalks 4–12 in. long

FRUIT Dry, reddish purple, opening at maturity, ⅛ in. long, 1-seeded

Vanillaleaf can be utilized in the garden as a groundcover as it forms large patches in suitable habitats. The leaves and stem come up separately from the rhizome, but the stem invariably comes up at the base of the leaf, and they look connected. The common name refers to the distinct vanilla fragrance given off by the leaves, particularly when dried.

Berberidaceae—barberry family
Vancouveria hexandra

white inside-out-flower, northern inside-out-flower

HABITAT Woodlands, forests, lowland to mid-montane

BLOOMS Spring, summer

DESCRIPTION Herbaceous perennial, rhizomatous, stem erect, leafless, inflorescence an open, many-branched cluster, flowers nodding, plants 8–15 in. tall

FLOWERS Parachute-like, sepals 6, petals 6, all white, bent back with tips curved, sepals larger than petals, stamens 6

LEAVES Basal only, 4–12 in. long, stalk hairy near base, blades usually twice divided into 3, leaflets heart-shaped and 3-lobed, resembling a duck's foot, hairy underneath, leaves early-deciduous, beginning to fall as the fruit matures

FRUIT Pod, glandular-hairy, seeds 1–6

White inside-out-flower grows from Washington to Northern California in shady forests and adapts well to shady gardens, forming a groundcover. The pods open before the seeds are mature, but they remain inside the pod and continue their maturation. Seeds of white inside-out-flower have a fleshy elaiosome and are dispersed by ants. The ants carry the seeds to their colony and feed the fleshy bit to their larvae.

Caryophyllaceae—pink family
Cerastium arvense

field chickweed, meadow chickweed

HABITAT Open slopes, meadows, forest openings, rocky areas, lowland to alpine

BLOOMS Spring, summer

DESCRIPTION Herbaceous perennial, usually hairy, taprooted or rhizomatous, stems creeping to erect, leafy, inflorescence an open, branched cluster at the stem tip, plants 2–12 in. tall

FLOWERS Saucer-shaped on slender stalks, sepals 5, lance-shaped, to ⅛ in. long, glandular-hairy, tips pointed, petals 5, heart-shaped, white, to ¼ in. long, tips rounded, stamens 10, styles 5

LEAVES Opposite, linear to lance-shaped, ¼–1 in. long, mostly hairy, edges smooth, tips pointed, often with smaller leaf bundles in the axil

FRUIT Capsule, oblong, curved to one side, seeds brown

Plants near the coast and at lower elevations are more densely hairy than montane specimens. Alpine chickweed (*C. beeringianum*), restricted to high elevations, looks much like field chickweed, but it lacks the smaller leaf bundles in the leaf axils, is densely hairy, and has wider, oblong leaves.

Caryophyllaceae—pink family
Moehringia macrophylla
(*Arenaria macrophylla*)

large-leaf sandwort, big-leaved sandwort

HABITAT Forests, forest openings, balds, rocky slopes, lowland to mid-montane

BLOOMS Spring, summer

DESCRIPTION Herbaceous perennial, patch-forming, rhizomatous, stems erect to trailing, hairy, inflorescence an open, few-flowered cluster at the stem tip, plants 2–10 in. tall

FLOWERS Saucer-shaped, stalked, sepals 5, ovate to lance-shaped, surfaces short-hairy, tips pointed, petals 5, white, oblong, tips rounded, petals slightly shorter or longer than the sepals, stamens 10, pistil 1, styles 3

LEAVES Opposite, stalkless, oval to lance-shaped, 1–2 in. long, short-hairy, edges smooth, tips pointed, basal leaves absent

FRUIT Capsule, round to egg-shaped, seeds few

Large-leaf sandwort is characterized by its opposite, pointed leaves topped with delicate white flowers. It grows in shady dry to mesic forests, in forest edges or openings, and in balds and rocky areas. Bluntleaf sandwort (*M. lateriflora*) is similar to large-leaf sandwort but has rounded sepal tips, petals much longer than the sepals, and rounded leaf tips.

Celastraceae—bittersweet family

Parnassia fimbriata

fringed grass-of-Parnassus

HABITAT Bogs, seeps, wet meadows, streambanks, mid-montane to alpine

BLOOMS Summer

DESCRIPTION Herbaceous perennial, nonhairy, roots fibrous, stems 1 to several, erect, inflorescence a single showy flower at the stem tip, plants 6–12 in. tall

FLOWERS Star-shaped, sepals 5, green, oval to egg-shaped, edges toothed to fringed, petals 5, white, wedge-shaped, to ½ in. long, lower edges with white, comb-like lobes, fertile stamens 5, interspersed with modified thick-lobed sterile stamens

LEAVES All basal except for one small bractlike leaf on the stem, blades kidney-shaped, ¾–1½ in. wide, bright green, stalks 1–4 in. long

FRUIT Capsule, egg-shaped, seeds many

Similar species Cascade grass-of-Parnassus (*P. cirrata* var. *intermedia*) has modified stamens with slender hair-like lobes with glandular tips rather than the thick lobes of fringed grass-of-Parnassus. It grows in similar habitats as fringed grass-of-Parnassus and is common in Oregon, while rare in Washington.

Cucurbitaceae—cucumber family
Marah oregana (*Marah oreganus*)

coastal manroot, bigroot

HABITAT Fields, floodplains, thickets, open hillsides, lowland

BLOOMS Spring

DESCRIPTION Herbaceous perennial vine with a tuberous woody root, stems climbing or trailing with branched, curling tendrils at the stem tips, flowers clustered or not in the leaf axils, flowers male or female, both types present on all plants, fruit gourd-like

FLOWERS Bell-shaped, white, with 5–8 spreading lance-shaped lobes, stamens 3, pistil 1, male flowers in a narrow cluster, female flowers solitary

LEAVES Alternate, stalked, blades hairy, maplelike, lobes 5–7, to 8 in. long

FRUIT Egg-shaped to oval with a pointy tip, fleshy but drying when mature, spiny, inedible, seeds several

Coastal manroot is in the same family as cucumbers and gourds. The name manroot comes from the resemblance seen between the shape of the large woody root and that of the human body. The scientific name *Marah* means bitter in Hebrew, a reference to the species' very bitter-tasting root.

Ericaceae—heath family
Cassiope mertensiana

white heather, Mertens' mountain heather, western moss heather

HABITAT Shrubfields, meadows, subalpine forests, subalpine to alpine

BLOOMS Summer

DESCRIPTION Evergreen perennial shrub, stems trailing to erect, mat-forming, hairy or not, flowers single in the leaf axils, plants 2–12 in. tall

FLOWERS Bell-shaped, to ¼ in. long, nodding on slender stalks, sepals egg-shaped, reddish, tips pointed, petals 5-lobed, white, lobes egg-shaped and spreading

LEAVES Opposite, scale-like, lance- to egg-shaped, overlapping and covering the stem, nonhairy, tips pointed, to ⅛ in. long

FRUIT Capsule, round, to ⅛ in. across

The white, bell-shaped flowers of white heather help the fruit mature by modulating the temperature within, keeping heat inside and wind out. Clubmoss mountain-heather (*C. lycopodioides*), rare in Washington and absent from Oregon, is smaller than white heather, has tufts of hair at the leaf tips, and grows in rock crevices at high elevations.

Ericaceae—heath family
Chimaphila menziesii

little prince's-pine, Menzies' pipsissewa

HABITAT Conifer forests, low to high montane

BLOOMS Summer

DESCRIPTION Evergreen subshrub, rhizomatous, stem erect, reddish, flowers 1–3 at the stem tip, plants 2–6 in. tall

FLOWERS Saucer-shaped, nodding on short stalks, sepals 5, to ¼ in. long, petals round, white to pinkish, to ¼ in. long, stamens 10, pistil 1

LEAVES Whorled or alternate, evergreen, blades oval to lance-shaped, stalked, shiny, nonhairy, edges smooth or toothed, tips pointed, 1–2½ in. long

FRUIT Capsule, round, seeds many, tiny

Little prince's-pine is endemic to western North America. Sometimes found in similar habitats is pipsissewa (*C. umbellata*), which is a bit larger, usually has more than 3 flowers per plant, and has sepals that are less than ⅛ in. long.

Ericaceae—heath family
Monotropa uniflora

Indian pipe, ghost plant

HABITAT Shady forests, lowland to mid-montane

BLOOMS Summer

DESCRIPTION Herbaceous perennial, nonphotosynthetic, roots fleshy, stems several, clustered, unbranched, the entire plant white to pinkish, turning black with age, flower nodding, solitary at the stem tip, plants 2–10 in. tall

FLOWERS Bell-shaped, white, about ½ in. long, sepals 5, shed early, petals 5, spoon-shaped with a sac-like base, stamens 10

LEAVES Alternate, linear to lance-shaped, ¼ in. long

FRUIT Capsule, roundish, ⅛ in. across

Indian pipe is a mycoheterotroph, a plant that obtains nutrients from fungi in the soil. The fungi in turn are associated with the roots of coniferous trees, forming what are called mycorrhizal associations. The tree-fungi relationship benefits both, with the fungus gaining sugars from the tree and the tree receiving minerals from the fungus. The benefit, if any, to the fungus from Indian pipe is unknown.

Hydrophyllaceae—waterleaf family
Hydrophyllum fendleri

Fendler's waterleaf

HABITAT Meadows, shrublands, forest openings, mid-montane to subalpine

BLOOMS Spring, summer

DESCRIPTION Herbaceous perennial, rhizomatous, stem 1, hairy, stem leaves large, blades to 9 in. long, inflorescence of branched, flat-topped clusters on stalks from the leaf axils, plants 6–30 in. tall

FLOWERS Bell-shaped, sepal lobes 5, linear, edges long-hairy, petals 5, white to purplish, to ⅓ in. long, stamens less than twice as long as the petals

LEAVES Alternate, stalked, blades longer than wide, divided into 7–11 leaflets, edges sharp-toothed, teeth 4–8 per side, tips pointed

FRUIT Capsule, globe-shaped, seeds 1–3

A key characteristic of waterleaf species is their showy stamens that are longer than the bell-shaped flowers. Western waterleaf (*H. occidentale*), native to Oregon but not found in Washington, is similar to Fendler's waterleaf but has leaflets with 4 or less rounded teeth per side and has globe-shaped flower clusters.

Hydrophyllaceae—waterleaf family
Hydrophyllum tenuipes

Pacific waterleaf, slender-stem waterleaf

HABITAT Mesic forests, floodplains, often in shade, lowland to mid-montane

BLOOMS Spring, summer

DESCRIPTION Herbaceous perennial, rhizomatous, stem 1, hairy, stem leaves large, blade to 5 in. long, inflorescence of branched, flat-topped clusters on stalks from the leaf axils, plants 6–30 in. tall

FLOWERS Bell-shaped, sepal lobes 5, linear, edges long-hairy, petals 5, cream, greenish white to blue or purple, to ¼ in. long, stamens more than twice as long as the petals

LEAVES Alternate, stalk present, blades about as long as wide, mostly palmately divided into 5 leaflets, sometimes 7–9, edges sharp-toothed, tips pointed

FRUIT Capsule, globe-shaped, seeds 1–3

Distinguish from Fendler's waterleaf (*H. fendleri*) by Pacific waterleaf's tendency to grow at lower elevations, having leaf blades about as long as wide, shorter petals not more than ¼ in. long, and stamens more than twice as long as the petals.

Lamiaceae—mint family
Clinopodium douglasii

yerba buena

HABITAT Coniferous forests, lowland to mid-montane

BLOOMS Spring, summer

DESCRIPTION Aromatic herbaceous perennial, sparsely hairy, rhizomatous, stems square, trailing, to 3 ft. long, rooting at the nodes, some branches erect, flowers single in the leaf axils

FLOWERS Tubular, short-stalked sepals hairy, ribbed, edges 5-toothed, petals 2-lipped, upper lip 2-lobed, lower lip 3-lobed, white to purplish-tinged, stamens 4

LEAVES Opposite, blades roundish to egg-shaped, either short-stalked or not, ¼–1¼ in. long, edges toothed, tips rounded

FRUIT Nutlet, 4 per flower

Plants in the mint family typically have square stems and opposite leaves. Yerba buena means "good herb" in Spanish. Teas made from its leaves have a minty flavor and were traditionally brewed by Native American communities, as well as by European explorers and settlers. Can make a good groundcover in the garden, prefers some shade and tolerates poorer soils.

Liliaceae—lily family
Clintonia uniflora

queen's cup, bead lily, bride's bonnet

HABITAT Mesic coniferous forests, floodplains, riparian edges, lowland to mid-montane

BLOOMS Spring, summer

DESCRIPTION Herbaceous perennial, rhizomatous, stem 1, hairy, flowers solitary at the stem tip, plants 6–10 in. tall

FLOWERS Bell-shaped, tepals 6, white to cream, lance-shaped, ½–1 in. long, stamens 6, pistil 1

LEAVES Basal leaves 2 or 3, blades oval to oblong, shiny green with parallel veins, 3–6 in. long, edges hairy, tips rounded or pointed

FRUIT Berry, round to egg-shaped, deep blue, seeds several

Colony-forming, queen's cup makes a good addition to wetter areas in shady gardens. The deep blue berry is not considered edible for humans but is consumed by birds and other wildlife.

Liliaceae—lily family
Erythronium montanum

avalanche lily

HABITAT Meadows, forest openings, mid-montane to alpine

BLOOMS Summer

DESCRIPTION Herbaceous perennial from a slender bulb, ephemeral, nonhairy, stem 1, erect, inflorescence of 1–3 showy flowers at the stem tip, blooms soon after snowmelt, plants 6–10 in. tall

FLOWERS Star-shaped, nodding, tepals 6, white to cream with yellow on inner surface near the base, spreading, egg-shaped, tips pointed, 1–2 in. long, stamens 6, anthers yellow

LEAVES Basal, 2, stalked, green, blades egg-shaped, edges smooth, tips pointed, 4–8 in. long

FRUIT Capsule, oblong, seeds many

Often blooms in large patches across high-mountain meadows. Avalanche lily relies on insects to pollinate their flowers and studies suggest that climate change may result in a mismatch between when the flowers bloom and pollinator availability.

Liliaceae—lily family
Erythronium oregonum

Oregon fawn lily, giant white fawn lily

HABITAT Gravelly prairies, rocky slopes, forests, lowland, rarely to mid-montane

BLOOMS Spring

DESCRIPTION Herbaceous perennial from a slender bulb, ephemeral, nonhairy, stem 1, erect, inflorescence of 1–3 showy flowers at the stem tips, plants 4–12 in. tall

FLOWERS Star-shaped, nodding, tepals 6, white to cream with yellow on inner surface at the base, spreading, lance-shaped, tips pointed, 1½ in. long, stamens 6, anthers white to yellow

LEAVES Basal, 2, pale green, mottled with brown, blades oval to lance-shaped, edges wavy, tips pointed, 4½–10 in. long

FRUIT Capsule, club-shaped, seeds many

Oregon fawn lily can usually be distinguished from other white-flowered *Erythronium* species by its strongly mottled leaves. It is known to hybridize with other *Erythronium* spp. where populations overlap.

Liliaceae—lily family
Prosartes hookeri (Disporum hookeri)

Hooker's fairybells, drops-of-gold

HABITAT Forests, lowland to mid-montane

BLOOMS Spring, summer

DESCRIPTION Herbaceous perennial, rhizomatous, stem 1, erect, branched, hairy, inflorescence of 2 or 3 nodding, stalked flowers at the branch ends, flowers often hidden beneath the leaves, plants 1–3 ft. tall

FLOWERS Bell-shaped, tepals 6, creamy white, oval, ¼–½ in. long, tips pointed, stamens 6, not hidden by tepals

LEAVES Alternate, stalkless, blades oval to egg-shaped, 2–6 in. long, the upper surface sparsely hairy, the lower densely so, veins parallel, tips pointed, basal leaves absent

FRUIT Berry, egg-shaped, red, seeds 4–6

Similar species Smith's fairybells (*P. smithii*) can be distinguished from Hooker's fairybells by its longer tepals, ½–1 in. long, with stamens hidden within the tepals, and its nonhairy upper leaf surfaces. Hooker's fairybells grows well in shady gardens with organic soil and will eventually form a clonal patch due to its rhizomatous habit.

Melanthiaceae—bunchflower family
Toxicoscordion venenosum
(*Zigadenus venenosus*)

meadow death camas

HABITAT Meadows, forest openings, sagebrush-steppe, lowland to mid-montane

BLOOMS Spring

DESCRIPTION Ephemeral herbaceous perennial from an egg-shaped bulb, stem erect, leaves grasslike, flowers in a stalked, dense cluster at the stem tip, plants 6–24 in. tall, toxic

FLOWERS Saucer- to bell-shaped, white to cream, 6-lobed, lobes lance- to egg-shaped, the inner 3 longer than the rest, stamens 6, styles 3

LEAVES Basal and alternate along the stem, blades linear, 3–12 in. long, becoming bractlike near the stem tip

FRUIT Capsule, cylindric, seeds many, light brown

The bulb and leaves of meadow death camas are poisonous to humans and livestock. Vegetatively it looks similar to and often grows with common camas (*Camassia quamash*), which is edible. In bloom they are easily separated by flower size and color. It is common for Native American communities that collect camas bulbs to sometimes weed out meadow death camas within collecting areas to prevent accidental poisoning.

Melanthiaceae—bunchflower family
Trillium ovatum

western trillium, Pacific trillium, western wakerobin

HABITAT Forests, streambanks, lowland to mid-montane

BLOOMS Spring

DESCRIPTION Herbaceous perennial, nonhairy, short-rhizomatous, stems 1 to several, erect, flowers solitary at the stem tips, leaves 3 in a whorl below, plants 4–17 in. tall

FLOWERS Star-shaped, sepals 3, green, oblong to lance-shaped, petals 3, white, turning pink to purplish with age, egg-shaped, edges wavy, tips pointed, stamens 6, stigmas 3

LEAVES Whorled, not stalked, blades egg- to diamond-shaped, 2–6 in. long and almost as wide, edges smooth, tips pointed, basal leaves absent

FRUIT Berry-like, seeds numerous

Western trillium can thrive in shady woodland gardens when planted in rich organic soil. Its seeds have a high germination rate; however, they grow slowly and will take several years to flower after seedling establishment. Brook trillium (*Pseudotrillium rivale*), found in the Siskiyou Mountains of Oregon, is similar to, but smaller than, western trillium, with stalked leaves and pink to purplish spots on its petals.

Melanthiaceae—bunchflower family
Xerophyllum tenax

beargrass, western turkeybeard

HABITAT Forests, rocky slopes, meadows, lowland to subalpine

BLOOMS Spring, summer

DESCRIPTION Herbaceous perennial, rhizomatous, forming clumps of wiry, grass-like basal leaf rosettes, the flowering stems up to 5 ft. tall, inflorescence a dense pyramidal cluster of stalked flowers near the stem tip, flowers open from the bottom up

FLOWERS Star-shaped, tepals 6, white, oblong, spreading, stamens 6, erect, longer than the tepals, styles 3

LEAVES Basal and alternate along the stem, linear, green, wiry, edges sharp-toothed, tips pointed, 6–24 in. long, stem leaves shorter than the basal leaves

FRUIT Capsule, seeds black, 6–24 per capsule

The wiry leaves of beargrass are gathered by Native Americans to make baskets and other items. A beargrass clump often consists of several rosettes growing close together from the short rhizome. A long-lived perennial, each rosette sends up a flowering stem only once. Beargrass resprouts after fire and benefits from the increased levels of light and water available in the postfire environment.

Montiaceae—springbeauty family
Claytonia perfoliata (Montia perfoliata)

miner's lettuce

HABITAT Rocky areas, forest openings, disturbed areas, lowland to mid-montane

BLOOMS Spring

DESCRIPTION Annual, taprooted, stems several, erect, green, inflorescence a narrow cluster of stalked flowers at the stem tip with a round cup-shaped leaf below, plants 2–14 in. tall

FLOWERS Saucer-shaped, sepals 2, oblong, petals 5, oblong, white to pinkish, to ¼ in. long, stamens 5, styles 3

LEAVES Basal leaves green, held erect, stalked, blades lance- to diamond-shaped, to 2 in. long, stem leaf a green cup-shaped disk below the inflorescence, ¼–4 in. across

FRUIT Capsule, seeds 1–3, shiny black, elaiosome present

Leaves of miner's lettuce are edible; the name originated with its use by miners as a salad green. It blooms while soils are moist in spring, then withers as soils dry and temperatures rise in summer. Similar species red miner's lettuce (*C. rubra*) can be distinguished by its reddish foliage and spreading, rather than upright basal leaves.

Montiaceae—springbeauty family
Claytonia sibirica (Montia sibirica)

candy flower, Siberian miner's lettuce

HABITAT Forests, shrublands, prefers shade, lowland to mid-montane

BLOOMS Spring, summer

DESCRIPTION Annual or short-lived perennial, taprooted or rhizomatous, stems several, flower clusters open, one to several at the stem tip with leafy bracts below, plants 2–16 in. tall

FLOWERS Saucer-shaped, stalked, sepals 2, petals 5, oblong, white, pink-striped, or deep pink tips notched, stamens 5, stigmas 3

LEAVES Basal and opposite along the stem, stalked or not, blades oval, lance-, or diamond-shaped, about as broad as long, ½–2 in. wide and to 3 in. long, tips pointed

FRUIT Capsule, seeds shiny black, elaiosome present

Stems, leaves, and flowers are edible and were used as a salad green by miners and settlers. The common name candy flower refers to the pink striping of the petals. Can be confused with broad-leaved springbeauty (*C. cordifolia*), which lacks bracts at the base of the flower stalks, is always perennial, and has white flowers.

Onagraceae—evening primrose family
Circaea alpina

enchanter's nightshade

HABITAT Mesic forests, meadows, riparian zones, lowland to mid-montane

BLOOMS Spring, summer

DESCRIPTION Herbaceous perennial, hairy, rhizomatous, stems erect, sometimes branched, inflorescence branched, with narrow clusters at the stem tip and in the leaf axils, plants 4–20 in. tall

FLOWERS Tiny, petals 2, sepals 2, less than ⅛ in. long, sepals whitish and bent back, petals white, 2-lobed, stamens 2, pistil 1

LEAVES Opposite, stalked, blades heart- to egg-shaped, 1–2 in. long, edges toothed, tips pointed

FRUIT Capsule, surface covered with hooked hairs, 1-seeded

Enchanter's nightshade thrives in dappled sun to shade in rich soil. Often becomes weedy in the garden. The hooked hairs of the fruit aid seed dispersal by attaching to the fur of passing animals.

Orchidaceae—orchid family
Goodyera oblongifolia

western rattlesnake-plantain, rattlesnake orchid

HABITAT Shady woodlands and forests, lowland to mid-montane

BLOOMS Summer

DESCRIPTION Herbaceous perennial, rhizomatous, stems erect, glandular-hairy, flowers in a narrow, dense cluster at the stem tip, plants 10–17½ in. tall

FLOWERS Hood-like, sepals 3, petals 3, greenish white, hood about ¼ in. long with a sac-like lip, tip bent outward, 1 sepal to each side, tips curled back, stamens and pistil fused into a column

LEAVES Basal only, evergreen, stalked, blades oval to lance-shaped, 1–3 in. long, dark green with a white stripe down the center and mottling on the sides, edges wavy, tips pointed

FRUIT Capsule, seeds tiny, numerous

The common name rattlesnake-plantain comes from the leaf surface looking a bit like a rattlesnake's scale pattern, while the leaf shape is similar to that of common plantain (*Plantago major*). Each orchid capsule contains thousands of minute seeds dispersed by the wind. The seeds form associations with fungi in the soil to gain nutrients needed for germination.

Orchidaceae—orchid family
Platanthera dilatata (Habenaria dilatata)

white bog orchid, scentbottle, bog candle

HABITAT Wetlands, ditches, wet meadows, lowland to subalpine

BLOOMS Summer

DESCRIPTION Herbaceous perennial, nonhairy, roots fibrous, stem erect, leafy, inflorescence a narrow, dense cluster at the stem tip, flowers showy, fragrant, plants 6–36 in. tall

FLOWERS Hood-like, white, sepals 3, petals 3, hood ⅛ in. long, lip pendant with a cylindric spur at the base, spur curved, ⅛–⅜ in. long

LEAVES Alternate, nonhairy, blades lance-shaped, ½–4 in. long, tips rounded or pointed

FRUIT Capsule, egg-shaped, seeds many

Three varieties of white bog orchid are recognized, and all are present in our area. In var. *albiflora* the spur is shorter than the lip, in var. *dilatata* the spur is as long as the lip, and in var. *leucostachys* the spur is noticeably longer than the lip.

Orobanchaceae—broomrape family
Castilleja parviflora var. *albida*

white small-flowered paintbrush, white mountain paintbrush

HABITAT Meadows, streambanks, shrubfields, subalpine to alpine

BLOOMS Summer

DESCRIPTION Herbaceous perennial, stems erect or curved at the base, unbranched, nonhairy to sparsely hairy, inflorescence brush-like at the stem tip, plants 8–15 in. tall

FLOWERS Showy bracts about as long as the sepals and petals, bracts oval to egg-shaped with narrower side lobes, soft-hairy, white to yellowish, rarely pink or magenta, sepals tubular, same color as bracts, petals greenish, tubular with upper hood and lip below, stamens 4

LEAVES Alternate, blades oval to lance-shaped, lobes 3–5, sparsely hairy, tips mostly pointed

FRUIT Capsule, seeds small, straw-colored

Small-flowered paintbrush has three varieties in our area. White small-flowered paintbrush, which has white bracts and sepals, grows in the North Cascade Mountains of Washington. Olympic Mountain paintbrush, var. *olympica*, has purple to magenta bracts and is endemic to the Olympic Mountains. Magenta paintbrush, var. *oreopola*, has magenta to dark red bracts and predominates in Oregon and southern Washington.

Oxalidaceae—oxalis family
Oxalis oregana

redwood sorrel, Oregon wood-sorrel, Oregon oxalis

HABITAT Forests, streambanks, lowland to mid-montane

BLOOMS Spring, summer

DESCRIPTION Herbaceous perennial, rhizomatous, leaves basal, stems several, brownish-hairy, leafless, flowers solitary, plants 4–10 in. tall

FLOWERS Cup-shaped, sepals 5, egg-shaped, hairy, petals 5, oval to egg-shaped, ½–1 in. long, white to pinkish with reddish lines, tips rounded, stamens 10, joined at the base into a tube

LEAVES Basal only, stalks brownish-hairy, blades divided into 3 heart-shaped leaflets, each leaflet up to 1¾ in. wide

FRUIT Capsule, egg-shaped

Great wood-sorrel (*O. trilliifolia*) looks somewhat similar to redwood sorrel, and it grows in similar habitats, but has several flowers per stem in a branched inflorescence and narrow capsules. Adapted to shade, leaflets of redwood sorrel fold up in direct sun to limit damage. It forms a dense groundcover in native habitats and adapts well to garden settings; however, it usually spreads aggressively, displacing other plants.

Polygonaceae—buckwheat family
Bistorta bistortoides (*Polygonum bistortoides*)

American bistort, western bistort

HABITAT Wet meadows, streambanks, wetlands, mid-montane to alpine

BLOOMS Spring, summer

DESCRIPTION Herbaceous perennial, rhizomatous, stems erect, flowers in a dense, cylindric cluster at the stem tip, plants 8–28 in. tall

FLOWERS Cup-shaped, tepals 5, white to pinkish, oblong, tips pointed, stamens 8, protruding beyond the tepal lobes, lower flowers not replaced by bulblets

LEAVES Basal with few, alternate stem leaves, stalked, blades elliptic to lance-shaped, 2–8 in. long, green, smooth above, whitish and sometimes hairy below, edges smooth, tips pointed

FRUIT Achene, 3-sided, yellowish brown

Alpine bistort (*B. vivipara*) can be confused with American bistort. Its range is mainly north of our area, but it does occur in northern Washington and eastern Oregon. Alpine bistort is shorter, up to 1 ft. tall, and the lower flowers are replaced with pinkish purple bulblets. Bulblets are vegetatively produced reproductive units, clones of the parent, able to become new plants.

Ranunculaceae—buttercup family
Anemone occidentalis (*Pulsatilla occidentalis*)

western pasqueflower, old man of the mountain, tow-headed baby

HABITAT Rocky slopes, meadows, mid-montane to alpine

BLOOMS Spring, summer

DESCRIPTION Stout perennial, densely hairy, taproot woody, branched, blooms soon after snowmelt, flowers solitary at the stem tips, plants 7¾–19½ in. tall

FLOWERS Saucer-shaped, petals absent, sepals 5–7(8), petal-like, creamy white to purplish-tinged, ½–1 in. long, stamens and pistils many

LEAVES Basal leaves stalked, palmately divided into 3 leaflets, leaflets divided into linear segments, with a whorled set of stem leaves at mid-length

FRUIT Achene, hairy, style persistent, feathery, elongates as the fruit matures, ¾–1 in. long

More often seen in fruit than in flower due to its early bloom. Wind disperses the seeds of western pasqueflower, the feathery styles allowing the achenes to be carried away. It contains compounds that may irritate or inflame the skin and other tissues.

Ranunculaceae—buttercup family
Caltha leptosepala

white marsh marigold, elkslip

HABITAT Marshes, seeps, and other wet habitats, subalpine to alpine

BLOOMS Spring, summer

DESCRIPTION Herbaceous perennial, fleshy, nonhairy, roots fibrous, stems erect, stem leaves 1 or none, flowers solitary at the stem tips, rarely 2 or more, plants 2–12 in. tall

FLOWERS Saucer-shaped, sepals petal-like, 7–12, white to greenish, outer surface may be bluish-tinged, oblong to oval, petals absent, stamens many, pistils 4–15

LEAVES Basal, stalked, blades arrow- to heart-shaped, to 4 in. long, up to 2 times longer than wide, edges smooth to toothed, tips rounded

FRUIT Pod, linear to oblong, nonhairy, seeds several

Blooms soon after snowmelt. White marsh marigold is considered a hybrid of twin-flowered marsh marigold (*C. biflora*) which grows in our area, and elkslip (*C. chionophila*), which does not. In contrast to white marsh marigold, twin-flowered marsh marigold has leaves about as long as wide and mostly has 2 flowers per stem.

Rosaceae—rose family
Aruncus dioicus

Sylvan goatsbeard, bride's feathers

HABITAT Streambanks, forest openings, roadsides, trail edges, lowland to subalpine

BLOOMS Spring, summer

DESCRIPTION Herbaceous perennial, rhizomatous, stems several, separate male and female plants, stems erect, flowers in branched clusters at the stem tips, plants 3–6½ ft. tall

FLOWERS Tiny, petals white, less than 1/16 in. long, male flowers with 15–20 white stamens

LEAVES Alternate, stalked, lower leaves larger and mostly 3 times pinnately divided, leaflets egg- to lance-shaped, 2–5 in. long, smooth above and hairy below, edges double toothed, tips long-pointed; upper leaves are smaller and less divided

FRUIT Pod, to ⅛ in. long, seeds few

The common name of the species derives from the resemblance of the flower cluster to a goat's beard. Sylvan goatsbeard adapts well to a woodland garden setting, needs some sun, is not drought tolerant, and is slow to establish from seed. It prefers soils that are higher in organic matter.

Rosaceae—rose family
Fragaria chiloensis

beach strawberry, coast strawberry

HABITAT Sand dunes, beaches, bluffs, coastal, lowland

BLOOMS Spring

DESCRIPTION Herbaceous perennial, mat-forming with runners, runners silky-hairy, stem leaves absent, inflorescence a branched cluster, stems 1–4 in. tall, often shorter than the basal leaves

FLOWERS Bowl-shaped, stalked, sepals 5, lance-shaped, silky-hairy, petals 5, roundish, white, to ½ in. long, stamens and pistils many, plants sometimes unisexual

LEAVES Basal, leathery, shiny green, blades divided into 3 leaflets, leaflets wedge- to egg-shaped, ½–1½ in. long, edges toothed, hairy below, leaf stalks to 4 in. long, reddish

FRUIT Berry, hairy, red, to ½ in. across

Beach strawberry can be used as a groundcover in the garden, preferably in full sun and well-drained soils. The commercial strawberry variety *Fragaria × ananassa* was a result of hybridization between beach strawberry and blueleaf strawberry (*F. virginiana*) in European gardens.

Rosaceae—rose family
Fragaria vesca

woodland strawberry, greenleaf strawberry

HABITAT Moist forest openings, streambanks, sandy areas, lowland to mid-montane

BLOOMS Spring

DESCRIPTION Herbaceous perennial, mat-forming with runners, runners short-hairy, stem leaves absent, inflorescence a branched cluster, stems 2–6 in. tall, as tall or taller than the basal leaves

FLOWERS Bowl-shaped, stalked, sepals 5, lance-shaped, silky-hairy, petals 5, roundish, white to pinkish, ⅓ in. long, stamens and pistils many, some plants unisexual

LEAVES Basal, thin, bright yellowish green, blades divided into 3 leaflets, leaflets oval to egg-shaped, ½–2½ in. long, hairy above and below, edges sharp-toothed, leaflet tip longer than or same size as the adjacent teeth, leaf stalks to 4 in. long, reddish

FRUIT Berry, cone-shaped, red, ½ in. across

Woodland strawberry works well as a groundcover in the garden, preferably growing in full sun to part shade in moist, well-drained soil. Everbearing cultivars of woodland strawberry are commonly sold by the horticulture trade.

Rosaceae—rose family
Fragaria virginiana

blueleaf strawberry, Virginia strawberry, mountain strawberry

HABITAT Forest openings, meadows, streambanks, disturbed areas, lowland to subalpine

BLOOMS Spring

DESCRIPTION Herbaceous perennial, mat-forming with runners, flowers in a branched, open cluster at the stem tips, stems 2–4½ in. tall, shorter than or equaling basal leaf height

FLOWERS Bowl-shaped, stalked, sepals 5, lance-shaped, petals 5, roundish, white to pinkish, to ½ in. long, stamens and pistils many

LEAVES Basal only, bluish green, blades divided into 3 leaflets, leaflets egg-shaped, 1–3 in. long, nonhairy above, silky-hairy below, edges toothed, leaflet tip shorter than adjacent teeth, stalks reddish

FRUIT Berry, red, ⅓ in. across

Blueleaf strawberry can function as a groundcover in garden settings, preferring full sun and sandy or gravelly soils. It grows in drier habitats than woodland strawberry. To tell the two species apart, look at the leaflet edges; the leaflet tip of blueleaf strawberry is shorter than the adjacent teeth, while the leaflet tip of woodland strawberry is longer than the adjacent teeth.

Rosaceae—rose family
Luetkea pectinata

partridgefoot, luetkea

HABITAT Meadows, streambanks, rocky areas, subalpine to alpine

BLOOMS Summer

DESCRIPTION Evergreen subshrub, rhizomatous, stems trailing, forming large clumps, flowering stems erect, 4–6 in. tall, leaf resembles a bird's foot, inflorescence a dense, rounded cluster at the stem tip

FLOWERS Saucer-shaped, stalked, sepals 5, hairy or not, lobes triangular, petals spoon-shaped, white, spreading, stamens 20, showy, pistils 4–6

LEAVES Shiny green, basal and alternate along the stem, stalked, blades fan-shaped, 3-lobed, lobes divided into 2 or 3 linear segments, tips pointed

FRUIT Pod, to ⅛ in. long, hairy

Partridgefoot is adapted to a short growing season. Its persistent leaves and rhizomatous habit help the plant thrive in areas with deep snowpacks that melt late in the season. It makes an attractive groundcover in gardens, preferring cooler sites with some shade and abundant moisture.

Rubiaceae—madder family
Galium aparine

cleavers, stickywilly, common bedstraw

HABITAT Disturbed areas, roadsides, forests, grassy slopes, beaches and other habitats, lowland to mid-montane

BLOOMS Spring

DESCRIPTION Opportunistic annual, taprooted, stems square, sparsely branched, trailing to climbing, with hooked hairs on the edges, inflorescence of small, branched clusters of 3–5 flowers in the leaf axils, plants 3–36 in. long

FLOWERS Tiny, cross-like, petals joined in a short tube, 4-lobed, white to greenish, stamens 4, styles 2

LEAVES Whorls of 6–8, blades linear to oblong, hooked-hairy, tips rounded with an abrupt sharp point, ⅓–1½ in. long

FRUIT Burr, 2-knobed, hooked-hairy, to ⅛ in. across, seeds 2

Cleavers often scrambles over adjacent plants and forms tangled mats of stems. The hooked hairs give it a rough texture and facilitates attachment to other plants and itself. The hooked hair of the fruit has a similar function, attaching to the fur of passing animals.

Saxifragaceae—saxifrage family
Boykinia occidentalis (*Boykinia elata*)

coastal brookfoam, western boykinia, slender boykinia

HABITAT Mesic forests, streambanks, pond edges, coastal, lowland to lower montane

BLOOMS Summer

DESCRIPTION Herbaceous perennial, rhizomatous, stems with reddish brown, soft hairs, often glandular, flower clusters branched, flat-topped, bracts not leaflike, flower stalks densely reddish glandular-hairy, plants 6–24 in. tall

FLOWERS Bell-shaped, sepals 5, nonhairy, lobes lance-shaped, petals 5, white, egg-shaped, narrowing toward the base, 2–3 times longer than the sepals

LEAVES Basal and alternate on the stem, basal and lower stem leaves stalked, blades heart-shaped, 1–3 in. wide, 5–7 lobed, tips pointed

FRUIT Capsule, seeds black

Two other species of *Boykinia* occur in our area, Sierra brookfoam (*B. intermedia*) and large boykinia (*B. major*), the latter not in Washington. Coastal brookfoam has petals 2–3 times longer than the sepals, while the other two species have shorter petals. In addition, large boykinia has saucer-shaped rather than bell-shaped flowers and the flower clusters of Sierra brookfoam are pyramidal rather than flat-topped.

Saxifragaceae—saxifrage family
Heuchera micrantha

small-flowered alumroot, crevice heuchera, crevice alumroot

HABITAT Rock crevices, rocky slopes, streambanks, lowland to subalpine

BLOOMS Spring, summer

DESCRIPTION Herbaceous perennial, rhizomatous, leaves mostly basal, stems 1 to several, slender, inflorescence a willowy, branched, open cluster of small flowers, plants 10–24 in. tall

FLOWERS Sepals bell-shaped with 5 lobes, glandular-hairy, petals 5, white, about twice as long as the sepals, stamens 5, stamens and style longer than sepals

LEAVES Stem leaves absent or few and small, basal leaves many, stalks hairy or not, blades kidney- to heart-shaped, mostly longer than wide, hairy, 5–7-lobed, edges toothed

FRUIT Capsule, seeds many, oval, not curved, black, short-spiny

Smooth alumroot (*H. glabra*) is similar to small-flowered alumroot but has basal leaves wider than long and is non-hairy. Small-flowered alumroot grows in shade or sun; it is often seen tenaciously perched on rock outcrops and in crevices. Cultivars of alumroot are often called coral bells.

Saxifragaceae—saxifrage family
Leptarrhena pyrolifolia

leatherleaf saxifrage

HABITAT Wet meadows and slopes, streambanks, seeps, mid-montane to alpine

BLOOMS Summer

DESCRIPTION Herbaceous perennial, rhizomatous, leaves mostly basal, leathery, stems erect, reddish, glandular-hairy, inflorescence a dense, branched flower cluster at the stem tip, plants 8–15 in. tall

FLOWERS Tiny, sepals and petals 5, sepals cup-shaped, lobed, petals white, twice as long as the sepals, stamens 10, longer than the petals

LEAVES Basal and alternate along the stem, evergreen, leathery, blades oval to egg-shaped with a short stalk, 1–6 in. long, upper surface shiny, dark green, edges toothed, teeth rounded, stem leaves few, much smaller, stalkless

FRUIT Pod, red, seeds many

Found on both sides of the Cascades in Washington, but in Oregon only at high elevations of the Cascade Mountains. You're more likely to see leatherleaf saxifrage with its bright red seedpods than in bloom. Leatherleaf saxifrage makes a good garden plant, growing well in wet areas.

Saxifragaceae—saxifrage family
Micranthes ferruginea (*Saxifraga ferruginea*)

rusty saxifrage

HABITAT Streambanks, seeps, wet rocky areas, lowland to alpine

BLOOMS Summer

DESCRIPTION Herbaceous perennial, root crown woody with short rhizomes, stems 1 to several, dark reddish brown, glandular-hairy, stem leaves lacking, inflorescence an open, branched cluster, flowers sometimes replaced by bulblets, plants 6–14 in. tall

FLOWERS Saucer-shaped, sepals 5, petals 5, sepals bent back, reddish brown, glandular-hairy, petals white, of 2 types, 3 wider with yellow dots at the base, the remaining 2 all-white, stamens 10

LEAVES Basal only, fleshy, hairy, blades spoon- to wedge-shaped, 1–4 in. long, edges irregularly toothed

FRUIT Capsule, green to reddish, seeds many

Rusty saxifrage was in the genus *Saxifraga* until taxonomists moved species that did not have stem leaves into the genus *Micranthes*. The bulblets are a form of vegetative reproduction; they fall to the ground and are able to develop into new plants, genetically identical to the parent.

Saxifragaceae—saxifrage family
Micranthes integrifolia (Saxifraga integrifolia)

whole-leaf saxifrage, grassland saxifrage, early saxifrage

HABITAT Prairies, grassy slopes, wet places, lowland to subalpine

BLOOMS Spring, summer

DESCRIPTION Herbaceous perennial, rhizomatous, stem 1, glandular-hairy, glands pink to purple, stem leaves lacking, axils of basal leaves with bulblets, inflorescence of branched, often dense clusters with a linear bract below, plants 4–12 in. tall

FLOWERS Sepals 5, petals 5, sepals lance-shaped, spreading to bent back, petals white, egg-shaped with rounded tips, stamens 10

LEAVES Basal only, fleshy, egg-shaped with a short stalk, densely hairy underneath, edges fringed with hair, toothed or not, tips rounded, ¾–2¾ in. long

FRUIT Capsule, reddish purple, seeds many, brown

One habitat type for whole-leaf saxifrage is remnant gravel prairie, such as those in South Puget Sound and Oregon's Willamette Valley. The rare Taylor's checkerspot butterfly is found in these prairies, with whole-leaf saxifrage one of the butterfly's key forage plants.

Saxifragaceae—saxifrage family
Micranthes tolmiei (Saxifraga tolmiei)

alpine saxifrage, Tolmie's saxifrage

HABITAT Meadows, streambanks, rocky slopes, subalpine to alpine

BLOOMS Summer

DESCRIPTION Mat-forming subshrub, root crown woody, vegetative stems trailing with overlapping, crowded leaves, flower stems erect, 1–3 in. tall, usually leafless, inflorescence a branched, few-flowered cluster or solitary

FLOWERS Saucer-shaped, sepals 5, petals 5, sepals oval to egg-shaped, spreading, petals white, longer than the sepals, oval to lance-shaped, tips pointed, stamens petal-like

LEAVES Alternate, succulent, blades lance- to spoon-shaped, edges smooth, sometimes fringed with hair at the leaf base, tips rounded

FRUIT Capsule, egg-shaped, seeds many, light brown

The cushion habit of alpine saxifrage helps it survive the harsh alpine environment with its deep snows, strong desiccating winds, and changes in temperature. Wind speed and temperature variation are lower close to ground level.

Saxifragaceae—saxifrage family
Saxifraga austromontana
(*Saxifraga bronchialis*)

spotted saxifrage, matted saxifrage, yellow-dot saxifrage

HABITAT Cliffs, talus slopes, rocky areas, mid-montane to alpine

BLOOMS Summer

DESCRIPTION Mat-forming perennial, taprooted, basal leaves dense, moss-like, stems erect, glandular-hairy, inflorescence a branched, open, flat-topped cluster, plants 2–5 in. tall

FLOWERS Bowl-shaped, sepal lobes 5, green, triangular, tips pointed, petals 5, oblong, white with yellow and reddish purple spots, tips rounded, stamens 10

LEAVES Evergreen, stiff, basal leaves persistent after withering, blades linear to lance-shaped, to ½ in. long, edges with stiff hairs, tips pointed, spiny, stem leaves alternate, smaller than the basal leaves

FRUIT Capsule, oblong, purplish, seeds dark brown

Similar species matted saxifrage (*S. vespertina*) has at times been considered a variety of spotted saxifrage. More common around Mount Rainier and south into Oregon, matted saxifrage has oblong or spoon-shaped leaves with rounded, spiny tips, and yellow to orange spots on the petals.

Saxifragaceae—saxifrage family
Tellima grandiflora

fringecup

HABITAT Forest edges, streambanks, trailsides, lowland to mid-montane

BLOOMS Spring, summer

DESCRIPTION Herbaceous perennial, with non-glandular and glandular hairs, short-rhizomatous, stems 1 to several, upright, stem leaves few, flowers in a long, narrow cluster near the stem tip, plants 1–2½ ft. tall

FLOWERS Bell-shaped, sepals 5-lobed, green, petals 5, greenish white to reddish, edges lobed, frilly, often curled around the bell lip, stamens 10

LEAVES Basal and alternate along the stem, stalks densely hairy, basal blades heart- to egg-shaped, 1–3 in. wide, shallowly 5–7 lobed, dull green, sparsely hairy, edges single or doubly toothed, stem leaves smaller

FRUIT Capsule, seeds many

Some fringecup populations have highly fragrant flowers and petals that don't curl around the bell. Once separated as fragrant fringecup (*T. odorata*), now they are considered a variation of *T. grandiflora*. Fringecup preferably grows in partial or full shade. The name *Tellima* is an anagram of *Mitella*, as it was originally thought to belong in the *Mitella* genus.

Saxifragaceae—saxifrage family
Tiarella trifoliata

foamflower, cut-leaved foamflower, triple sugar scoop

HABITAT Streambanks, forests, lowland to mid-montane

BLOOMS Spring, summer

DESCRIPTION Herbaceous perennial, glandular-hairy, rhizomatous, stems 1 to several, erect, slender, inflorescence an elongated, branched flower cluster near the stem tip, plants 6–18 in. tall

FLOWERS Bell-shaped, nodding, tiny, sepal lobes 5, white, 1 larger than the rest, glandular-hairy, petals 5, linear, white, stamens 10, unequal in length

LEAVES Basal and alternate on the stem, glandular-hairy, blades heart-shaped, ½–3 in. long, 3–5 lobed or divided into 3 leaflets, these again lobed, edges toothed, stem leaves smaller than basal leaves

FRUIT Capsule, scoop-shaped, few-seeded, seeds shiny black

Foamflower's flower clusters remind some people of flecks of sea-foam. It has three varieties: var. *unifoliata* with 1 undivided, lobed leaf, var. *trifoliata* with leaves divided into 3 moderately lobed leaflets, and var. *laciniata* that has 3 deeply lobed leaflets. Foamflower grows well in shady woodland gardens, preferring organic soils and moist conditions.

Valerianaceae—valerian family
Valeriana sitchensis

Sitka valerian, mountain heliotrope

HABITAT Meadows, streambanks, open forests, mid-montane to alpine

BLOOMS Summer

DESCRIPTION Herbaceous perennial, nonhairy, roots fibrous, rhizomatous or not, stems square, unbranched, erect, leafy, flowers in a dense, round to flat-topped cluster at the stem tip, plants 1–4 ft. tall

FLOWERS Trumpet-shaped, to ¼ in. long, fragrant, white to pinkish, petal lobes 5, less than half as long as the tube, stamens 3, pistil 1, protruding, sepals divided into many feathery segments, enlarging in fruit

LEAVES Opposite, stalked, blades pinnately divided into 3–7 leaflets, terminal leaflet larger, egg-shaped, the rest oval, edges toothed, tips pointed, basal leaves few and smaller

FRUIT Achene, egg-shaped, with feathery tuft at the tip

Similar species Scouler's valerian (*V. scouleri*) grows from low to middle elevations, only reaches 2 ft. tall, and has many basal leaves that are larger than those of the stem. Pollinated by bees and flies, Sitka valerian also attracts butterflies.

Yellow Flowers

Apiaceae—parsley family
Lomatium nudicaule

barestem biscuitroot, barestem desert parsley, pestle lomatium

HABITAT Grassy slopes, meadows, shrub-steppe, dry forests, lowland to mid-montane

BLOOMS Spring

DESCRIPTION Aromatic herbaceous perennial, nonhairy, taprooted, foliage bluish green, stems 1 to several, erect, inflorescence umbrella-shaped, rays of the umbel unequal, each ray with a cluster of small flowers at the tip, plants 8–36 in. tall

FLOWERS Tiny, stalked, sepals absent, petals 5, yellow, stamens 5, styles 2, bisexual or male only

LEAVES Mostly basal, stalked, blades pinnately divided 1–3 times, leaflets oblong to egg-shaped, 1–3½ in. long

FRUIT Dry, oblong to oval, ribbed with a winged edge, 2-seeded

Barestem biscuitroot is a long-lived perennial that tolerates disturbances like fire, resprouting afterward from the root system. It provides forage for wildlife and hosts larvae of several butterfly species. It was believed that barestem biscuitroot was pollinated by many types of insects, but recent research has shown that its primary pollinators are solitary, ground-nesting mining bees in the *Andrenidae* family.

Apiaceae—parsley family
Lomatium utriculatum

spring gold, fine-leaf desert parsley, foothill lomatium

HABITAT Coastal bluffs, prairies, rocky areas, low elevations

BLOOMS Spring

DESCRIPTION Herbaceous perennial, taprooted, short-hairy or nonhairy, stems erect, leafy, inflorescence umbrella-shaped, rays of the umbel each with a cluster of small flowers at the tip, with egg-shaped bracts beneath, plants 4–24 in. tall

FLOWERS Tiny, sepals absent, petals 5, yellow, stamens 5, styles 2, flowers bisexual or male only

LEAVES Fernlike, alternate on the stem and basal, stalked, shiny green, blades divided into many linear leaflets, each to ¼ in. long, tips pointed

FRUIT Dry, oval to egg-shaped, ribbed, edge thin-winged, 2-seeded

Spring gold is among the earliest plants to bloom in spring. Distinguish spring gold from the rare Bradshaw's desert parsley (*L. bradshawii*) by the latter's lack of stem leaves and a thick, rather than thin, wing on the fruit. Bradshaw's desert parsley grows in remnant wet meadows in the Willamette Valley in Oregon and in Clark County, Washington.

Apiaceae—parsley family
Sanicula crassicaulis

Pacific sanicle, Pacific snakeroot

HABITAT Prairies, coastal bluffs, open forests, meadows, lowland to lower montane

BLOOMS Spring

DESCRIPTION Herbaceous perennial, taprooted, stem 1, erect, leafy, leaves leathery, inflorescence branched, with several stalked, dense, round clusters, plants 10–48 in. tall

FLOWERS Small, petals 5, yellow or purplish, flowers bisexual or male, stamens 5

LEAVES Alternate, all stalked except the upper stem leaves, blades 1–5 in. long, 3–5 lobed or divided into 3 leaflets, edges toothed, basal leaves similar in shape to stem leaves

FRUIT Bur, roundish, with prickles curved at tips, 2-seeded

Pacific sanicle has two varieties: var. *crassicaulis* with yellow flowers and leaf blades about as long as wide, and var. *tripartita* with purplish flowers and leaf blades longer than wide. Fruit of Pacific sanicle sticks to the fur of passing animals, dispersing the seeds away from the parent plant.

Araceae—arum family
Lysichiton americanus

yellow skunk cabbage, swamp lantern

HABITAT Shallow streams, swamps, lake or pond edges, lowland to mid-montane

BLOOMS Winter, spring

DESCRIPTION Herbaceous perennial with a skunky odor, rhizomatous, stem absent, floral structures emerge first, the flowers in a dense, oblong cluster surrounded by a large yellow bract, leaves large, fleshy, plant 1–2 ft. tall

FLOWERS Tiny, tepals 4, yellowish green, flower cluster partially enclosed by a large, bright yellow, egg-shaped bract

LEAVES Basal only, 1–3 ft. long, stalked, blades lance- to egg-shaped, bright green, fleshy, edges wavy, tips pointed

FRUIT Berrylike, ⅛ in. wide

Another name for this species is swamp lantern, as the yellow bracts can seem like flickering flames as they emerge from the dark wet soil. Skunk cabbage flowers generate heat; temperatures of about 70 degrees Fahrenheit have been recorded within the flowers while the ambient air was near freezing. The skunky odor attracts early pollinators like beetles and flies.

Asteraceae—aster family
Arnica latifolia

broadleaf arnica, mountain arnica

HABITAT Meadows, forest openings, rocky areas, streambanks, mid-montane to alpine

BLOOMS Spring, summer

DESCRIPTION Herbaceous perennial, glandular and hairy, rhizomatous, stems 1 to few, erect, leafy, inflorescence 1 to several stalked heads at the stem tip, plants 4–20 in. tall

FLOWERS Bracts of the head lance-shaped, sparsely to densely hairy, glandular, both ray and disk flowers present, rays showy, yellow, disk flowers yellow

LEAVES Opposite, 2–4 pairs along the stem, stalked or not, blades lance- to egg-shaped, edges toothed, tips pointed, 1–4½ in. long, basal leaves triangular to heart-shaped

FRUIT Achene, nonhairy near the base, with a tuft of hair at the top

Key characters of arnica species are their opposite leaves and having only a few largish flower heads per stem. Arnica preparations are known to relieve pain and decrease inflammation. Creams or gels are typically made with arnica flowers. As with any medicine, consult your medical professional before use.

Asteraceae—aster family
Eriophyllum lanatum

Oregon sunshine, woolly sunflower, woolly yellow daisy

HABITAT Rocky areas, meadows, forest openings, lowland to subalpine

BLOOMS Spring, summer

DESCRIPTION Herbaceous perennial, woolly-hairy, taprooted, stems several, erect to trailing, inflorescence a solitary head at the stem tip, plants 4–24 in. tall

FLOWERS Bracts of the head lance- to egg-shaped, in one row, erect, woolly-hairy, both ray and disk flowers present, rays oval, yellow to golden yellow, ¼–¾ in. long, disk flowers yellow

LEAVES Alternate or opposite, blades lance-shaped, grayish green, divided into leaflets or not, woolly-hairy, ¼–3 in. long

FRUIT Achene, hairy or not, sometimes glandular

A variable species, Oregon sunshine is adapted to dry, sunny habitats. It has dense woolly hair on its foliage that traps water vapor close to the surface, thus reducing water loss through transpiration. Oregon sunshine grows well in rock or dry meadow gardens, spreads easily, and attracts a variety of pollinators. Plant it in sandy to rocky well-drained soil in sunny spots.

Asteraceae—aster family
Grindelia integrifolia

Puget Sound gumweed, Willamette Valley gumweed

HABITAT Rocky shorelines, marshes, headlands, wet meadows, roadsides, lowland

BLOOMS Summer, fall

DESCRIPTION Herbaceous perennial, resinous, taprooted, stems several, erect, leafy, inflorescence of branched clusters of stalked heads at the stem tips and the leaf axils, plants 8–30 in. tall

FLOWERS Bracts of the head linear to lance-shaped in several rows, sticky, tips spreading to curling, both ray and disk flowers present, rays 10–35, yellow, disk flowers yellow

LEAVES Alternate along the stem and basal, blades lance-shaped, basal up to 6 in. long, stem leaves 1–3 in. long, surfaces glandular-hairy, edges smooth to toothed, tips pointed

FRUIT Achene, with 2 or 3 curled bristles at the top

Growing throughout Puget Sound and the Willamette Valley, the bright yellow heads of gumweed bloom all summer into fall. The sticky resin found on the plant deters herbivory and minimizes water loss.

Asteraceae—aster family
Senecio integerrimus

western groundsel, tall western groundsel, mountain butterweed

HABITAT Forests, meadows, shrub-steppe, lowland to subalpine

BLOOMS Spring, summer

DESCRIPTION Herbaceous perennial, hairs stiff or cobwebby, roots fibrous, stem 1, erect, flowers clustered in heads, stalked and several at the stem tip, the central head often larger, plants 8–24 in. tall

FLOWERS Bracts of the head in a single row, lance-shaped, usually black-tipped, both ray and disk flowers present, rays yellow, cream, or absent, disk flowers yellow or creamy white

LEAVES Basal and alternate on the stem, 2–9 in. long, stalked, blades oval, lance-, or heart-shaped, edges smooth or toothed, tips pointed, upper stem leaves shorter, stalkless

FRUIT Achene, with tuft of hair at the top

Western groundsel is native to the western United States and Canada, extending east to the Midwest. It has two varieties in our area: var. *ochroleucus* with yellowish white rays, and var. *exaltatus* that has either bright yellow rays or is rayless with discoid heads.

Asteraceae—aster family
Senecio triangularis

arrowleaf groundsel, arrowleaf ragwort, bog groundsel

HABITAT Wetlands, streambanks, wet meadows, lower montane to alpine

BLOOMS Spring, summer

DESCRIPTION Herbaceous perennial, roots fibrous, stems several, erect, leaves similar in size along the stem, inflorescence a flat-topped cluster of stalked heads at the stem tip, plants 1–5 ft. tall

FLOWERS Bracts of the head erect, in a single row, lance-shaped, hairy or not, black-tipped, both ray and disk flowers present, rays strap-shaped, yellow, disk flowers yellow

LEAVES Basal and alternate on the stem, stalked, blades triangular to arrowhead-shaped, 1½–8 in. long, nonhairy above, sparsely hairy below, edges toothed, tips pointed

FRUIT Achene, ribbed, nonhairy, with tuft of hair at the top

Arrowleaf groundsel is usually relatively easy to identify due to its distinctive leaf shape and preference for wet habitats. The flowers are pollinated by a variety of insects including bumblebees, bees, butterflies, beetles, and flies.

Asteraceae—aster family
Solidago lepida (Solidago gigantea)

western Canada goldenrod, late goldenrod, smooth goldenrod

HABITAT Meadows, fields, shrub thickets, lowland to montane

BLOOMS Summer, fall

DESCRIPTION Herbaceous perennial, rhizomatous, stems many, erect, inflorescence a pyramidal branched cluster of stalked heads at the stem tip, plants 1–5 ft. tall

FLOWERS Bracts of the head lance-shaped, tips pointed, outer ones shorter than the inner, both ray and disk flowers present, ray flowers 10–16, strap-shaped, yellow, disk flowers yellow

LEAVES Alternate, stalked or not, blades oval to lance-shaped, 1½–6 in. long, leaves largest near the middle of the stem, edges smooth or toothed, tips pointed

FRUIT Achene, short-hairy, with a tuft of white hair at tip

Western Canada goldenrod grows well in garden settings, preferring full sun. It will form a clump over time, spreading through its rhizomes. Its abundant flowers are an important source of nectar and pollen for bumblebees, butterflies, and other insects as fewer species bloom late in the growing season.

Asteraceae—aster family
Wyethia angustifolia

narrowleaf mule's ears, narrowleaf wyethia

HABITAT Prairies, meadows, lowland to mid-montane

BLOOMS Spring, summer

DESCRIPTION Herbaceous perennial, taprooted, stems long-hairy, leaning to erect, leafy, inflorescence usually a solitary, sunflower-like head at the stem tip, plants 6–36 in. tall

FLOWERS Bracts of the head linear to lance-shaped, ¼–1 in. long, hairy, edges fringed with hair, tips pointed, both ray and disk flowers present, rays yellow, strap-shaped, ½–1 in. long, disk flowers yellow

LEAVES Basal and alternate along the stem, blades oval to lance-shaped, 6–18 in. long, surfaces hairy, edges smooth or toothed, tips pointed, stem leaves smaller than the basal leaves

FRUIT Achene, short-hairy

Narrowleaf mule's ears is rare in Washington, found in remnant Puget Sound prairies. It is threatened by invasive species and habitat loss. The range of narrowleaf mule's ears extends south through Oregon to central California. *Wyethia* spp. are called mule's ears as the size and shape of the basal leaves are similar to the ears of mules.

Crassulaceae—stonecrop family
Sedum oreganum

Oregon stonecrop

HABITAT Rock outcrops, talus slopes, gravelly areas, lowland to subalpine

BLOOMS Summer

DESCRIPTION Succulent perennial, nonhairy, rhizomatous, stems several, curved at the base becoming erect, stems vegetative or flowering, inflorescence a dense, flat-topped cluster at the stem tip, plants 2–8 in. tall

FLOWERS Star-shaped, sepals 5, green, tips pointed, petals 5, bright yellow, joined at the base, lobes lance-shaped, to ½ in. long, tips long-pointed, stamens 10

LEAVES Alternate, fleshy, evergreen, blades spoon-shaped, ¼–¾ in. long, flattened, green to reddish green, wider and crowded at the tips of vegetative stems, narrower and overlapping, but not crowded, on flowering stems

FRUIT Pod, erect, 5 per flower, seeds numerous

Leaves of stonecrops and other plants can turn reddish under bright sun. The reddish color comes from a type of leaf pigment called anthocyanin. Studies suggest that anthocyanin protects leaves from sun and water stress.

Crassulaceae—stonecrop family
Sedum spathulifolium

broadleaf stonecrop, Pacific stonecrop

HABITAT Coastal cliffs and bluffs, forest openings, rock outcrops, lowland to montane

BLOOMS Spring

DESCRIPTION Succulent perennial, nonhairy, rhizomatous, stems several, erect to curved at the base, leaves in basal rosettes, grayish green, flower clusters open and flat-topped at the stem tips, plants 3–8 in. tall

FLOWERS Star-shaped, sepals 5, tips rounded, petals 5, bright yellow, lance-shaped, tips pointed, stamens 10

LEAVES Alternate on the stem and basal, fleshy, evergreen, spoon- to egg-shaped, ¼–¾ in. long, flattened, grayish green to reddish with a white, waxy powdery coating, basal leaves crowded in circular rosettes, stem leaves spreading

FRUIT Pod, spreading, seeds numerous

The term stonecrop is thought to refer to the species' habit of frequently living on rock, including stone walls. Broadleaf stonecrop might be confused with Oregon stonecrop (*S. oreganum*), which has pointy, long-tapered petal tips, erect pods, and green leaves, whereas broadleaf stonecrop has none of these traits.

Ericaceae—heath family

Pterospora andromedea

pinedrops, woodland pinedrops

HABITAT Forests, woodlands, lowland to mid-montane

BLOOMS Summer

DESCRIPTION Herbaceous nonphotosynthetic perennial, roots nodular, forming a ball-like mass, stems 1 to several, unbranched, reddish brown, glandular-hairy, inflorescence an elongated cluster of nodding, stalked flowers at the stem tip, plants 1–3 ft. tall

FLOWERS Urn-shaped, to ¼ in. long, sepals 5, lance-shaped, reddish, glandular-hairy, petals 5-lobed, light yellow to cream, stamens 10, pistil 1

LEAVES Alternate, bractlike, lance-shaped to linear, crowded at the stem base

FRUIT Capsule, reddish brown, glandular-hairy, seeds many

Pinedrops is a mycotrophic species, parasitizing mycorrhizal fungi that are connected to tree roots. It grows in shady forests and woodlands. The name *Pterospora* is from the Greek words *pteron* (wing) and *sporos* (seed), referring to the morphology of its seeds. The netlike wing of the seed facilitates dispersal by air currents. Pinedrops stems are fleshy but harden as they dry, often persisting into the next year. The stems work well in dried plant arrangements.

Liliaceae—lily family
Erythronium grandiflorum

glacier lily, yellow fawn-lily

HABITAT Meadows, slopes, forest openings, lowland to subalpine

BLOOMS Spring, summer

DESCRIPTION Herbaceous perennial from a slender bulb, ephemeral, nonhairy, stems erect, leafless, inflorescence of 1 to several stalked flowers at the stem tip, plants 6–12 in. tall

FLOWERS Star-shaped, nodding, tepals 6, pale to golden yellow, lance-shaped, 1–1¼ in. long, curling outward, tips pointed, stamens 6, anthers white, yellow, or red

LEAVES Basal only, blades lance-shaped, shiny green, edges smooth, tips pointed, 4–8 in. long

FRUIT Capsule, oblong, seeds many

Glacier lily is among the first species to bloom during the growing season, as its emergence is tied to snowmelt and soil temperature. Black and grizzly bears often dig up and consume the bulbs. While the bear activity decreases plant abundance, in the longer term glacier lily populations increase due to higher soil nitrogen levels that spur plant growth and seed production.

Liliaceae—lily family
Streptopus amplexifolius

clasping twisted-stalk

HABITAT Streambanks, forests, shrub thickets, lowland to subalpine

BLOOMS Spring, summer

DESCRIPTION Herbaceous perennial, rhizomatous, stems erect, branched, leafy, flowers solitary, rarely 2, nodding on bent stalks from the leaf axils, flowers beneath the leaves, plants 1½–4 ft. tall

FLOWERS Bell-shaped, tepals lance-shaped, greenish white to yellowish green, tips pointed and curved outward, stamens 6, pistil 1

LEAVES Alternate, blades lance- to egg-shaped, 2–4½ in. long, glossy green, clasping the stem, veins parallel, edges smooth or minutely toothed, tips pointed

FRUIT Berry, yellow to red, many-seeded

Clasping twisted-stalk may be confused with Hooker's fairy-bells (*Prosartes hookeri*), which has 1–3 bell-shaped flowers at the tips of the branches rather than in the leaf axils. Two other species of twisted-stalk occur in our area: rosy twisted-stalk (*S. lanceolatus*), which has tepals that are rose or white with reddish purple streaks, and small twisted-stalk (*S. streptopoides*), which has shorter, unbranched stems and greenish tepals with a purplish tinge.

Nyctaginaceae—four-o'clock family
Abronia latifolia

yellow sand verbena, coastal sand verbena

HABITAT Coastal beaches, sand dunes

BLOOMS Spring, summer

DESCRIPTION Mat-forming perennial herb, taprooted, stems trailing and much branched, often buried in sand, usually glandular pubescent

FLOWERS Trumpet-shaped, yellow to orangish, flower tube length and lobe diameter each ¼–½ in., lobes notched, gathered in clusters with 5 egg-shaped bracts beneath, clusters stalked at the leaf nodes

LEAVES Opposite, blades ovate to triangular, sometimes kidney-shaped, edges usually smooth, ⅜–2⅓ in. long, grayish green, glandular-hairy or nonhairy, succulent

FRUIT Achene, diamond-shaped, 4–5-winged, ¼–½ in. long

Pink sand verbena (*A. umbellata* var. *acutalata*), rare in Washington and Oregon, grows in similar habitats along the outer coast. Sand verbena leaves are sticky, becoming coated with sand. The sand has protective effects, deterring insect predators and reducing leaf temperatures by reflecting light.

Nymphaeaceae—water lily family
Nuphar polysepala

yellow pond lily, spatterdock

HABITAT Ponds, lake shallows, slow-moving streams, lowland to montane

BLOOMS Spring, summer

DESCRIPTION Aquatic herbaceous perennial, with long, thick (1–3 in. wide) rhizomes, stems fleshy, 3–6½ ft. long, basal leaves floating, flower solitary, floating or held slightly above the water surface

FLOWERS Bowl-shaped, sepals 9, outer sepals smaller, leathery and greenish, inner sepals petal-like, bright yellow to reddish, egg- to wedge-shaped, 1–2 in. long, tips slightly notched, petals small, lance-shaped, stamens many, reddish to purple

LEAVES Basal only, floating, leathery, green, blades heart-shaped, 4–15½ in. long, tips pointed

FRUIT Ribbed capsule, egg-shaped, seeds many, released in jelly-like mass

Yellow pond lily is closely related to white-flowered American water-lily (*Nymphaea odorata*). Yellow pond lily has sepals much larger than the petals, while flowers of American water-lily have petals larger than the sepals. Not native to the west coast, American water-lily has been introduced to Oregon and Washington and is considered established in Washington.

Orobanchaceae—broomrape family
Pedicularis bracteosa

bracted lousewort, towering lousewort, wood betony

HABITAT Forests, meadows, open slopes, mid-montane to alpine

BLOOMS Spring, summer

DESCRIPTION Herbaceous perennial, roots tuberous, fibrous, stems 1 to several, erect, unbranched, leaves fernlike, inflorescence a dense, spirelike cluster at the stem tip, plants 8–36 in. tall

FLOWERS Hoodlike, sepals hairy, tubular, 5-lobed, lobes linear, top lobe shorter than the rest, petals 2-lipped, ½–¾ in. long, yellow, reddish, purplish-tinged, or dark red to purple, upper lip hoodlike, lower lip 3-lobed

LEAVES Basal and alternate along the stem, blades lance-shaped, 3–10 in. long, pinnately divided into linear to lance-shaped lobes, lobe edges toothed to doubly toothed, tips pointed, basal leaves sometimes absent

FRUIT Capsule, curved, nonhairy

Bracted lousewort and other *Pedicularis* species are considered hemiparasites as they obtain nutrients through a combination of photosynthesis and parasitism. Hemiparasites have specialized rootlike structures called haustoria that penetrate the host plant's root system, forming a bridge between the two species.

Phrymaceae—lopseed family
Erythranthe guttata (Mimulus guttatus)

yellow monkeyflower, seep-spring monkeyflower

HABITAT Seeps, streambanks, meadows, headlands, rock crevices, roadsides, lowland to mid-montane

BLOOMS Spring, summer

DESCRIPTION Herbaceous perennial, rhizomatous, stems square, erect, hairy, inflorescence of paired, stalked flowers from the upper leaf axils forming a loose cluster, plants 6–24 in. tall

FLOWERS Two-lipped, sepals green, tubular with 5 teeth, the top tooth longer than the rest, petals tubular, 2-lipped, yellow with maroon spots, upper lip 2-lobed, the lower lip larger, 3-lobed, ¼–¾ in. long, stamens 4

LEAVES Opposite, stalked or not, blades roundish, oval, or egg-shaped, to 5 in. long, 1 to 2 times longer than wide, edges variously toothed to lobed, tips rounded

FRUIT Capsule, seeds many

There are several other monkeyflower species with yellow flowers in our area. Plants with the following combination of traits are likely to be yellow monkeyflower: a perennial habit, maroon spots on the lower lip, top sepal tooth longer than the rest, a roundish leaf shape, and nonglandular hairs.

Ranunculaceae—buttercup family
Ranunculus occidentalis

western buttercup

HABITAT Meadows, prairies, coastal bluffs, forests, lowland to subalpine

BLOOMS Spring, summer

DESCRIPTION Herbaceous perennial, roots fibrous, stems 1 to several, erect to reclining, branched, hairy, with basal and stem leaves, inflorescence an open, branched cluster of stalked flowers, plants 6–18 in. tall

FLOWERS Bowl-shaped, petals mostly 5 but can be up to 8, bright yellow, oblong, longer than the sepals, tips rounded, sepals 5, hairy, bent back, and shed early

LEAVES Basal and alternate on the stem, stalked, blades 3-lobed, about 1 in. long, lobes wedge-shaped, each again shallowly lobed to toothed, hairy, upper stem leaves linear, bractlike

FRUIT Achene, flattened with a short beak, beak curved or not

Meadow buttercup (*R. acris*), an introduced species from Europe, can be confused with western buttercup. It has several differences including flowers with egg-shaped rather than oblong petals and sepals that are spreading rather than bent back.

Rosaceae—rose family
Drymocallis glandulosa
(Potentilla glandulosa)

sticky cinquefoil

HABITAT Meadows, roadsides, streambanks, forest openings, lowland to subalpine

BLOOMS Spring, summer

DESCRIPTION Herbaceous perennial, glandular-hairy, stems erect, reddish, flower clusters branched, open, at stem tips and in upper leaf axils, plants 6–36 in. tall

FLOWERS Disk-shaped, stalked, sepals 5 with smaller bracts in between, petals 5, creamy white to yellow, egg-shaped to roundish, slightly shorter than or equal to the sepals, stamens and pistils many, style spindle-shaped

LEAVES Basal and alternate along the stem, blades pinnately divided into 5–9 leaflets, oblong to egg-shaped, edges doubly toothed, sparsely to densely hairy

FRUIT Achene, reddish brown

Sticky cinquefoil was previously part of the *Potentilla* genus; it was reclassified based on DNA analysis and the morphology of the anther and style. *Drymocallis* spp. have styles that attach to the bottom half of the ovary and have anthers with 1 pollen chamber, while *Potentilla* spp. have styles attached near the top of the ovary and anthers with 2 pollen chambers.

Rosaceae—rose family
Geum macrophyllum

large-leaved avens

HABITAT Forest and trail edges, roadsides, meadows, lowland to subalpine

BLOOMS Spring, summer

DESCRIPTION Herbaceous perennial, hairy, rhizomatous, stems 1 to several, both basal and stem leaves present, inflorescence a branched cluster at the stem tip and in upper leaf axils, plants 1–2 ft. tall

FLOWERS Saucer-shaped, sepals 5, triangular and bent back, petals 5, roundish to egg-shaped, to ¼ in. long, bright yellow, stamens and pistils numerous

LEAVES Basal leaves divided, up to 11 in. long, leaflets unequal in size, leaflet at the leaf tip maple-like, much larger than rest, tips rounded, edges toothed, stem leaves alternate, blades divided into 3 similar-sized lobes, lobes lance-shaped, edges toothed, tips pointed

FRUIT Achene, hairy, style persistent, forms hook-like twist near the tip

Large-leaved avens tolerates disturbance and prefers edge habitats, resulting in its frequent appearance along trails and roadsides. Found throughout western and northern United States, Canada, and east to Japan and Kamchatka.

Rosaceae—rose family
Potentilla anserina ssp. *pacifica*
(*Potentilla pacifica*)

Pacific silverweed

HABITAT Salt marshes, sand dunes, beaches, coastal, low elevations

BLOOMS Spring, summer

DESCRIPTION Herbaceous perennial, spreading by runners (stolons), flower stalks leafless, flowers solitary at the stem tip, plants 1–4 in. tall

FLOWERS Bowl-shaped, sepals 5, triangular, long-hairy, with bracts between the sepals, petals 5, oblong, ¼–½ in. long, lemon yellow, stamens 25–30, pistils many

LEAVES Basal, stalked, blades pinnately divided into several paired leaflets with one at the tip, 4–12 in. long, leaflets oblong to egg-shaped, to 1 in. long, upper surface green, the lower surface white woolly-hairy, edges toothed

FRUIT Achene, oval, reddish brown

Pacific silverweed forms clonal patches, sending out runners that root at the nodes and form new shoots. Nutrients can be transferred from one shoot of Pacific silverweed to another as the runners form a connected network, a trait called clonal integration. This sharing of nutrients aids survival of shoots throughout the patch.

Rosaceae—rose family
Potentilla flabellifolia

fan-leaf cinquefoil, high mountain cinquefoil

HABITAT Meadows, streambanks, rocky slopes, mid-montane to alpine

BLOOMS Summer

DESCRIPTION Herbaceous perennial, rhizomatous, stems erect, basal leaves many, stem leaves 1 or 2, inflorescence an open, branched cluster, flowers 1–5, plants 6–12 in. tall

FLOWERS Bowl-shaped, sepals 5, triangular, hairy, often glandular, with bracts between sepals, petals 5, heart-shaped, ¼ in. long, golden yellow, tips notched, stamens 20, pistils many

LEAVES Stalks of the basal leaves 2–3 times as long as the leaf blade, blades divided into 3 leaflets, leaflets wedge- to fan-shaped, ½–1 in. long, edges toothed, teeth rounded and uneven, stem leaves similar but smaller

FRUIT Achene

The golden yellow flowers of fan-leaf cinquefoil attract many insects with their nectar and pollen, including bees, butterflies, beetles, and moths. In fruit, the flower transforms into a bowl full of rounded achenes, the seeds scattering when the bowl tips in the wind or when jostled by a passing animal.

Rosaceae—rose family
Potentilla gracilis

fivefinger cinquefoil, slender cinquefoil, graceful cinquefoil

HABITAT Forests, meadows, shrub-steppe, lowland to subalpine

BLOOMS Summer

DESCRIPTION Herbaceous perennial, taprooted, stems several, hairy, branched, basal leaves many, stem leaves 1–2, inflorescence an open, branched, flat-topped cluster with few to many flowers, plants 1–2½ ft. tall

FLOWERS Bowl-shaped, sepals 5, lance-shaped, hairy, sometimes glandular, with bracts between the sepals, petals 5, bright yellow, heart-shaped, tips notched, stamens 20, pistils many

LEAVES Basal and alternate along the stem, stalked, blades palmately divided, leaflets 7–9, wedge- to lance-shaped, 1–3 in. long, woolly-hairy beneath, edges toothed to lobed, stem leaves smaller

FRUIT Achene, greenish

Fivefinger cinquefoil has several recognized varieties. It tolerates saline soils and does not form clonal patches. The invasive nonnative sulphur cinquefoil (*P. recta*) can be confused with fivefinger cinquefoil. Tell them apart as sulphur cinquefoil has more than 2 stem leaves, few basal leaves that are not woolly-hairy beneath, and is patch-forming.

Violaceae—violet family
Viola glabella

stream violet, pioneer violet, smooth yellow violet

HABITAT Streambanks, forests, lowland to subalpine

BLOOMS Spring, summer

DESCRIPTION Herbaceous perennial, rhizomatous, stems 1 to several, arching to erect, only the upper stem leafy, flowers single, stalked from the leaf axils, plants 2–15 in. tall

FLOWERS Spurred, petals 5, to ½ in. long, both surfaces lemon yellow, spur short, lower 3 petals purple-lined, stamens 5, style hairy at tip

LEAVES Basal and alternate along the stem, stalked, blades heart-shaped, 2–3½ in. long and about as wide, surfaces hairy or not, edges toothed, teeth tips rounded, leaf tips pointed

FRUIT Capsule, nonhairy, seeds dark brown

Violets are among the earliest plants to flower during the growing season. Distinguish steam violet from two other yellow-flowered species, evergreen violet (*V. sempervirens*) and round-leaved violet (*V. orbiculata*), both with mostly basal foliage and only 2–4 in. tall. Stream violet is taller and has stem leaves.

Violaceae—violet family
Viola orbiculata

round-leaved violet, dark woods violet

HABITAT Streambanks, seeps, forests, mid-montane to alpine

BLOOMS Spring, summer

DESCRIPTION Herbaceous perennial, rhizomatous, stems erect, leafy, basal leaves persistent, flowers solitary from the leaf axils, plants 2–3½ in. tall

FLOWERS Spurred, petals 5, to ½ in. long, both surfaces lemon yellow, spur short, lower 3 petals purple-lined, upper 2 sometimes purple-lined as well, stamens 5, style hairy at the tip

LEAVES Basal and alternate along the stem, stalked, blades round to heart-shaped, ½–2 in. long and wide, surfaces nonhairy, edges round-toothed, tips rounded

FRUIT Capsule, oval, seeds brown

Round-leaved violet is closely related to evergreen violet (*V. sempervirens*). Evergreen violet has runners and purple-blotched, hairy leaves, while round-leaved violet has neither trait and usually grows at higher elevations. Violet capsules open like a spring, scattering seed away from the parent plant. Seed is also dispersed by ants that carry it away into their colony, attracted by the seed's fleshy elaiosome.

Orange Flowers

Asteraceae—aster family
Agoseris aurantiaca

orange agoseris, orange false dandelion, slender agoseris

HABITAT Wetlands, meadows, open forests, disturbed areas, montane to subalpine

BLOOMS Summer

DESCRIPTION Herbaceous perennial, taprooted, hairy or not, stem erect, exudes milky juice when cut, head inflorescence, solitary at the stem tip, plants 4–24 in. tall

FLOWERS Bracts of the head lance-shaped, edges hairy, all ray flowers, rays usually deep orange, occasionally pink or yellow

LEAVES Basal only, lance-shaped, edges smooth or toothed, tips rounded or pointed, 2–14 in. long

FRUIT Achene with a slender beak, beak topped with a tuft of hair

Orange agoseris has two varieties: var. *aurantiaca* with orange rays that can turn purplish pink when fading, found in Oregon and Washington, and var. *carnea* with pink rays, which is only known from Washington. Seeds of orange agoseris are dispersed largely by wind, held aloft by the aerodynamics of the hair tuft at the seed top.

Caprifoliaceae—honeysuckle family
Lonicera ciliosa

orange honeysuckle, western trumpet

HABITAT Forest openings, edge habitats, shrubfields, lowland to mid-montane

BLOOMS Spring, summer

DESCRIPTION Woody vine, stems climbing or trailing, to 20 ft. long, leaves opposite, inflorescence a dense cluster at stem and branch ends, with an oval to cup-shaped leaf beneath the flower cluster

FLOWERS Trumpet-shaped, orange to reddish, 1–1½ in. long, floral tube 3–4 times longer than the lobes, stamens 5

LEAVES Opposite, blades oval, 1½–4 in. long, stalk short or absent, edges fringed with hair, tips pointed or rounded

FRUIT Berry, orange to red, about ½ in. across, inedible

Orange honeysuckle grows well in gardens with rich, well-drained soil, preferring partial shade but can tolerate full sun. The flowers attract bees and hummingbirds while the berries, although considered inedible for people, are readily eaten by birds.

Liliaceae—lily family
Lilium columbianum

Columbia lily, small-flowered tiger lily

HABITAT Open slopes, edge habitats, forest openings, lowland to subalpine

BLOOMS Spring, summer

DESCRIPTION Herbaceous perennial from an egg-shaped bulb, nonhairy, stem erect, leaves whorled to alternate along the stem, inflorescence a branched, open cluster of stalked, showy flowers at the stem tip, plants 2–4 ft. tall

FLOWERS Bell-shaped, nodding, not fragrant, yellowish to reddish orange with darker spots, tepals 6, curled back, lance-shaped, about 2 in. long, stamens 6

LEAVES Whorled, 6–9 per whorl, those of the upper stem often alternate, shiny green, lance-shaped, tips pointed, 1½–4½ in. long

FRUIT Capsule, to 1½ in. long

Columbia lily is pollinated by hummingbirds and butterflies. In Oregon it may be mistaken for the rare western lily (*L. occidentale*) or leopard lily (*L. pardalinum*). Both of these species are rhizomatous instead of bulb-based and their tepals vary in color from base to tip, while those of Columbia lily are one shade throughout.

Papaveraceae—poppy family
Eschscholzia californica

California poppy

HABITAT Grassy meadows, gravelly or rocky open areas, roadsides, disturbed areas, lowland to mid-montane

BLOOMS Spring, summer

DESCRIPTION Annual or herbaceous perennial, taprooted, stems 1 to several, nonhairy, inflorescence of solitary stalked flowers in leaf axils or at the stem tip, plants 4–20 in. tall

FLOWERS Bowl-shaped, sepals 2, deciduous as the petals open, petals 4, wedge-shaped, yellow to bright orange, ¼–1½ in. long, stamens many, pistil 1

LEAVES Basal and alternate along the stem, fernlike, stalked, blades divided several times, leaflets trident-shaped

FRUIT Capsule, linear, seeds brown or black

California poppy is considered native to Oregon but introduced north of the Columbia Gorge in Washington. A variable species, it spreads readily by seed, forming large drifts in suitable habitat. California poppy flowers are sensitive to sunlight, opening in sunny weather and closing at night and under cloudy skies.

Pink and Red Flowers

Amaryllidaceae—amaryllis family
Allium acuminatum

taper-tip onion

HABITAT Rocky areas, meadows, shrub-steppe, forest openings, lowland to mid-montane

BLOOMS Spring, summer

DESCRIPTION Aromatic herbaceous perennial from an egg-shaped bulb, outer coat net-patterned, stem erect, nonhairy, leafless, flowers in a rounded cluster at the stem tip, plants 4–12 in. tall

FLOWERS Vase-shaped, stalked, tepals 6, light to purplish pink, sometimes white, lance-shaped, the outer 3 tepals wider and longer than the inner, tips pointed and curled back, stamens 6

LEAVES Basal, blades linear, round to somewhat flattened, tips pointed, 3–11½ in. long

FRUIT Capsule, seeds black

Taper-tip onion is edible with an oniony aroma and can be abundant in suitable habitats. Distinguish from similar species slim-leaf onion (*A. amplectens*) that has 6 similar-sized tepals with straight tips. Also similar looking is Blue Mountain onion (*A. dictuon*), rare and endemic to the Blue Mountains of Washington. Unlike taper-tip onion, Blue Mountain onion is rhizomatous, forming new bulbs each year and has straight rather than curled tepal tips.

Amaryllidaceae—amaryllis family

Allium cernuum

nodding onion

HABITAT Rocky areas, meadows, forest openings, sandy areas, lowland to mid-montane

BLOOMS Spring, summer

DESCRIPTION Herbaceous perennial from a bulb, stems usually 1, erect, bulbs several, oblong and short-rhizomatous at the base, ¼–1 in. long, outer bulb coats grayish to brown with elongated narrow cells in lines, flowers in a nodding cluster at the stem tip, plants 3½–19½ in. tall

FLOWERS Bell-shaped, nodding, tepals 6, pink or white, oval to egg-shaped, tips rounded, about ⅛ in. long, stamens 6 and longer than the tepals, flowers stalked

LEAVES Basal, linear, flattened, 3½–9½ in. long, edges smooth to toothed

FRUIT Capsule, seeds black

The species name *cernuum* comes from the word cernuous, meaning drooping or nodding, referring to the habit of the flower cluster. Nodding flowers are an adaptation to discourage insect visitors other than bees. Edible.

Asteraceae—aster family
Antennaria microphylla (*Antennaria rosea*)

rosy pussytoes, rosy everlasting, small-leaf pussytoes

HABITAT Balds, meadows, forest openings, rocky slopes, lowland to alpine

BLOOMS Spring, summer

DESCRIPTION Herbaceous mat-forming perennial, grayish-hairy, separate male- and female-flowered plants, stoloniferous, stems erect, inflorescence a flat-topped cluster at the stem tip, plants 4–12 in. tall

FLOWERS Bracts of the head in overlapping shingled rows, bracts pink to rose, white, or yellow, rays absent, disk flowers whitish

LEAVES Basal and alternate along the stem, grayish green, densely woolly-hairy, edges smooth, tips pointed, ¼–1½ in. long, basal leaves many, lance- to spatula-shaped, stem leaves linear

FRUIT Achene, smooth or with small, rounded bumps

In alpine habitats rosy pussytoes may be confused with alpine pussytoes (*A. alpina*), which has brownish green to black bracts of the floral head. Many pussytoe species produce seeds at least partially through apomixis, without fertilization of the ovule. Seeds produced through apomixis are genetically the same as the parent plant.

Asteraceae—aster family
Cirsium edule

edible thistle, Indian thistle

HABITAT Meadows, riparian edges, forest openings, rocky slopes, lowland to high elevation

BLOOMS Summer

DESCRIPTION Herbaceous biennial to short-lived perennial, taprooted, not rhizomatous, stems erect, woolly-hairy, inflorescence a solitary head at the branch and stem tips, stalked or not, plants 1–6½ ft. tall

FLOWERS Bracts of the head woolly-hairy, 1–2 in. high, all disk flowers, pink to violet, style evident, longer than the petals

LEAVES Basal and alternate along the stem, to 1½ ft. long, blades lance-shaped, edges lobed to toothed and spiny, surfaces nonhairy to sparsely hairy

FRUIT Achene, brown, nonhairy, topped with a tuft of hair

Stems are fleshy and edible when peeled. Edible thistle attracts bumblebees, butterflies, beetles, and hummingbirds. The seeds are eaten by smaller birds such as finches. Edible thistle is a monocarpic perennial, meaning it only flowers once and then dies. It may persist as a rosette of basal leaves for a few years prior to developing flowers.

Convolvulaceae—morning glory family
Calystegia soldanella (*Convolvulus soldanella*)

beach morning glory, beach bindweed, coast morning glory

HABITAT Beaches, coastal sand dunes, low elevations

BLOOMS Spring

DESCRIPTION Fleshy perennial vine, rhizomatous, non-hairy, stems prostrate, up to 3 ft. long, often buried in sand, flowers stalked, solitary from the leaf axils, with heart-shaped bracts beneath, often covering the sepals

FLOWERS Funnel-shaped, sepals 5-lobed, divided nearly to the base, lobes oblong to egg-shaped, ½ in. long, petals tubular, pink to purplish with white stripes, stamens 5, pistil 1

LEAVES Alternate, fleshy, round to kidney-shaped, ½–1½ in. long, stalks 1–3 times longer than the blade, tips rounded or notched, edges smooth

FRUIT Capsule, roundish, about ½ in. long

Clonal mats of beach morning glory bind sand in place, helping stabilize beaches and sand dunes. The funnel-shaped flower attracts insects and shades the reproductive structures from the sun, preventing overheating. Its seeds float, and remain viable after long periods in seawater, facilitating long-range dispersal.

Ericaceae—heath family
Chimaphila umbellata

pipsissewa, western prince's-pine

HABITAT Conifer forests, lowland to mid-montane

BLOOMS Summer

DESCRIPTION Evergreen subshrub, rhizomatous, stems erect, green or reddish, often branched, inflorescence a cluster of 3–10 nodding, stalked flowers at the stem tip, plants 4–12 in. tall

FLOWERS Saucer-shaped, nodding on short stalks, sepals 5, less than ⅛ in. long, petals egg-shaped, pinkish to rose, to ⅜ in. long, stamens 10, pistil 1

LEAVES Whorled, evergreen, stalked, blades lance-shaped, 1¼–3 in. long, shiny green, nonhairy, edges smooth or toothed, tips pointed

FRUIT Capsule, round, with many tiny seeds

Pipsissewa is a circumboreal species found in shady forests. Distinguish it from the closely related little prince's-pine (*C. menziesii*), which is smaller with wider, oval leaves, and usually has 1–3 flowers. Pipsissewa contains a number of bioactive phytochemicals that researchers are studying for their potential in treating disease.

Ericaceae—heath family
Phyllodoce empetriformis

pink mountain-heather, pink mountain-heath

HABITAT Meadows, rocky slopes, high montane to alpine

BLOOMS Summer

DESCRIPTION Perennial shrub, mat-forming, stems branched, somewhat spreading to erect, leaves needlelike, crowded, inflorescence a cluster of 1 to several flowers on glandular-hairy, pinkish stalks up to 1 in. long at the stem tip, plants 4–15 in. tall

FLOWERS Bell-shaped, nodding to erect, ¼ in. long, sepals 5, egg-shaped, pinkish, edges hairy, petal bell pink to rose, nonhairy, lobes 5, tips curled outward, stamens 10

LEAVES Alternate, evergreen, linear, ¼–½ in. long, dark green, tips blunt or pointed

FRUIT Capsule, globe-shaped, glandular-hairy, seeds many

Distinguish pink mountain-heather from similar species yellow mountain-heather (*P. glanduliflora*) by the latter's yellow to white, glandular-hairy, urn-shaped flowers and glandular-hairy sepals. The two species form the hybrid *P.* ×*intermedia* when growing close to one another. The hybrids have pale pink urn-shaped flowers.

Fabaceae—pea family
Lathyrus nevadensis

Sierra pea, purple peavine

HABITAT Forests, meadows, grassy slopes, lowland to subalpine

BLOOMS Spring, summer

DESCRIPTION Herbaceous perennial, rhizomatous, stems climbing or erect, clusters of 2–7 stalked flowers from the leaf axils, plants 6–30 in. tall

FLOWERS Pea-like, 2-lipped, ½–1 in. long, bluish or reddish purple, pinkish, or rarely white, upper lip often darker than the lower lip, sepals hairy, 5-lobed, stamens 10, style hairy on one side

LEAVES Alternate, stalked, blades pinnately divided into oval to egg-shaped leaflets, ¾–2½ in. long, tendril present, sometimes reduced to a bristle

FRUIT Pod, nonhairy, 1–2¾ in. long

Wild peas (*Lathyrus* spp.) can sometimes be confused with the vetches (*Vicia* spp.) as both groups are viny with similar-shaped flowers and leaves. To distinguish wild peas from vetches, look closely at the style. The style of wild peas are hairy on one side, like a toothbrush, while vetch styles are hairy all around, like a bottlebrush.

Iridaceae—iris family

Olsynium douglasii

grass-widow, satinflower, purple-eyed grass-widow

HABITAT Rocky areas, woodlands, vernal wetlands, lowland to mid-montane

BLOOMS Winter, spring

DESCRIPTION Herbaceous perennial, roots fibrous, stems 1 to several, unbranched, leaves grasslike, inflorescence of 1–3 nodding, stalked flowers at the stem tip, plants 4–12 in. tall

FLOWERS Bell-shaped, to ¾ in. long, tepals 6, lance- to egg-shaped, light to dark reddish purple, satiny, tips rounded or pointed, stamens 3, joined at the base, pistil 1, stigmas 3-lobed

LEAVES Grasslike, alternate on the stem, linear, dark green, 2–6 in. long, tips pointed, basal leaves reduced, bractlike

FRUIT Capsule, egg-shaped, seeds brown

Blooming early in the growing season, grass-widow often grows in seasonal wetlands that dry up by summer. Ephemeral, the aboveground parts wither after the fruit matures. Grass-widow has two varieties: var. *inflatum* has an inflated, globe-shaped stamen tube, and var. *douglasii* has a nonglobe-shaped stamen tube. It makes an attractive addition to rock gardens.

Lamiaceae—mint family
Stachys cooleyae
(*Stachys chamissonis* var. *cooleyae*)

Cooley's hedge-nettle, great hedge-nettle

HABITAT Swamps, streambanks, ditches, shrub thickets, lowland to mid-montane

BLOOMS Summer

DESCRIPTION Herbaceous perennial, hairy, rhizomatous, stems square, erect, usually unbranched, leafy, inflorescence of tiered flower clusters at the stem tip, plants 2–5 ft. tall

FLOWERS Two-lipped, rose to magenta, hairy, petal tube ½–1 in. long, upper lip rounded, lower lip larger, 3-lobed with white mottling, sepal tube glandular-hairy, lobes 5, spine-tipped, stamens 4

LEAVES Opposite, stalked, blades heart- to egg-shaped, 2–6 in. long, hairy on both sides, edges toothed, teeth rounded, tips rounded

FRUIT Nutlet, 4 per flower

With its square stems, opposite leaves, and 2-lipped flowers, Cooley's hedge-nettle is a typical plant in the mint family (Lamiaceae). Similar species Mexican hedge-nettle (*S. mexicana*) is shorter, 1–3 ft. tall, and has smaller pink to magenta flowers, with the petal tube ¼–½ in. long.

Linnaeaceae—twinflower family
Linnaea borealis

twinflower

HABITAT Forests, forest openings, slopes, lowland to alpine

BLOOMS Spring, summer

DESCRIPTION Perennial subshrub, spreads through aboveground runners, stems woody at the base, hairy, sometimes glandular, inflorescence a pair of nodding flowers on short stalks, plants to 4 in. tall

FLOWERS Fragrant, nodding on a short stalk, trumpet-shaped, ¼–½ in. long, pink to whitish, petal lobes 5, rounded, sepals hairy, stamens 4

LEAVES Evergreen, opposite, blades egg-shaped to round, ¼–1 in. long, dark green and shiny, nonhairy, or hairy on the veins and edges, edges few-toothed or smooth

FRUIT Dry, 1-seeded, glandular-hairy

Twinflower works well as a groundcover in gardens, can grow in sun or shade, and prefers well-drained soils. The genus *Linnaea* is named after Carolus Linnaeus, a Swedish botanist who in the 1700s formalized the binomial naming system still used today.

Montiaceae—springbeauty family
Claytonia lanceolata

western springbeauty, lanceleaf springbeauty

HABITAT Grassy slopes, meadows, forests, shrub-steppe, lowland to alpine

BLOOMS Spring, summer

DESCRIPTION Herbaceous perennial from a bulblike corm, nonhairy, stems 1 to several, basal leaves present but withering early, flowers in an open, often 1-sided cluster, plants 2–8 in. tall

FLOWERS Saucer-shaped, stalked, sepals 2, petals 5, white to pink, often pinkish-lined, sometimes yellow, oblong to lance-shaped, ¼–½ in. long, tips notched, stamens 5, styles 3

LEAVES Basal leaves stalked, lance-shaped, stem leaves opposite, stalkless, lance- to egg-shaped, 1–3 in. long, edges smooth, tips pointed

FRUIT Capsule, egg-shaped, seeds shiny black with elaiosome

Western springbeauty seeds have elaiosomes, fleshy bits that attract ants. The ants aid seed dispersal as they carry the seeds back to their colony. Similar species broad-leaved springbeauty (*C. cordifolia*) is rhizomatous and has heart-shaped leaves. The rare Pacific lance-leaved spring-beauty (*C. multiscapa* ssp. *pacifica*), found in Washington's Olympic Mountains, has stalked stem leaves and unnotched petals.

Montiaceae—springbeauty family
Montia parvifolia

littleleaf montia, littleleaf miner's lettuce

HABITAT Rock outcrops, streambanks, shorelines, lowland to mid-montane

BLOOMS Spring, summer

DESCRIPTION Herbaceous perennial, nonhairy, rhizomatous and stoloniferous, stems several, leaves fleshy, edible, bulblets in some leaf axils, inflorescence an open cluster of stalked flowers at the stem tips, plants 4–12 in. tall

FLOWERS Funnel-shaped, sepals 2, petals 5, ¼–½ in. long, strap-shaped, tips notched, white to pink, veins deep pink, stamens 5

LEAVES Basal and alternate along the stem, stalked, blades egg- to spoon-shaped, ¼–2¼ in. long, tips pointed, stem leaves smaller than the basal leaves

FRUIT Capsule, egg-shaped, seeds 2, shiny black

Littleleaf montia can be incorporated into moister garden landscapes and establishes well. It spreads readily and may crowd out other plants due to its rhizomatous and stoloniferous habit, a trait to consider when selecting a planting location.

Onagraceae—evening primrose family
Chamaenerion angustifolium (Chamerion angustifolium, Epilobium angustifolium)

fireweed

HABITAT Open slopes, roadsides, disturbed areas, meadows, lowland to subalpine

BLOOMS Spring, summer

DESCRIPTION Herbaceous perennial, rhizomatous, patch-forming, stems erect, rarely branched, leafy, inflorescence a spirelike cluster at the stem tip, plants 3–10 ft. tall

FLOWERS Trumpet-shaped, deep rose pink to purple, sepals and petals 4, petals egg-shaped, ¼–¾ in. long, sepals lance-shaped, stamens 8, stigmas 4-lobed

LEAVES Alternate, blades lance-shaped, 2–8 in. long, green with a white central vein, edges smooth, tips pointed

FRUIT Capsule, podlike, to 3 in. long, seeds many, with a tuft of silky hair at the top

Fireweed seeds are light and easily carried by the wind, dispersing far from the parent plant. The seeds readily germinate in areas that have burned or are otherwise disturbed. Fireweed rapidly forms large patches in such places, creating a sea of rosy pink flowers, admired by humans and visited by hummingbirds and bees in search of nectar.

Onagraceae—evening primrose family
Epilobium ciliatum

common willowherb, Watson's willowherb, ciliate willowherb

HABITAT Lakeshores, streambanks, roadsides, meadows, forest openings, lowland to mid-montane

BLOOMS Summer

DESCRIPTION Herbaceous perennial, hairy, taprooted, stems erect, branched, with open, branched flower clusters at the stem and branch tips, plants 1–2 ft. tall

FLOWERS Funnel-shaped, sepals 4, lance-shaped, petals 4, egg-shaped, white, pink, or rose, to ½ in. long, tips notched, stamens 8, stigma not lobed

LEAVES Opposite, basal leaf rosettes often present, 1–4½ in. long, blades lance- to egg-shaped, usually hairy, edges toothed

FRUIT Capsule, linear, ½–3 in. long, glandular-hairy, seeds many, with a hair tuft at the top

Common willowherb occurs throughout most of North America, in southern South America, and temperate parts of Asia. Its seeds are dispersed by wind, the hair tuft acting as a parachute carrying seeds away from the parent plant. The name willowherb comes from the similarity of its leaf shape, long and slender, to that of many willows (*Salix* spp.).

Orchidaceae—orchid family
Calypso bulbosa

fairy slipper, calypso orchid, deer's-head orchid

HABITAT Mesic forests, organic soils, lowland to mid-montane

BLOOMS Spring

DESCRIPTION Herbaceous perennial, ephemeral, with bulblike corm and fibrous roots, nonhairy, stem erect with few translucent bracts, flowers solitary at the stem tip, plants 2–8 in. tall

FLOWERS Slipper-shaped, sepals 3, sepals and 2 petals lance-shaped, erect, deep pink, ½–1 in. long, sometimes twisted, 3rd petal slipper-shaped, main section of the slipper white with pink stripes on the sides, pink spots around the opening with white bristle-like hair within

LEAVES Basal, blades oval to egg-shaped, 1–2 in. long, emerges in fall and withers after the orchid blooms in spring

FRUIT Capsule, oval, seeds tiny, many

Fairy slippers in the area covered here are var. *occidentalis*. The other variety, var. *americana*, has yellow bristles on the slipper opening and occurs east of the Cascades in northern Washington. Seed of fairy slipper forms beneficial associations with mycorrhizal fungi, improving seed germination and survival.

Orchidaceae—orchid family
Corallorhiza maculata

spotted coralroot, summer coralroot

HABITAT Forests, often in deep shade, lowland to mid-montane

BLOOMS Spring, summer

DESCRIPTION Herbaceous perennial, parasitic, rhizomatous, stems purplish to reddish brown, rarely yellow, inflorescence a narrow, open cluster of short-stalked flowers at the stem tip, plants 8–16 in. tall

FLOWERS Hoodlike, sepals 3, lance-shaped, reddish brown, purplish, or rarely yellow, curved, 3-nerved, to ¼ in. long, petals 3, 2 similar to the sepals, the 3rd liplike, oval to egg-shaped, white with wine-red spots, to ¼ in. long, edges lobed, tip rounded, stamens and pistil fused into a curved column

LEAVES Reduced to alternate membranous bracts

FRUIT Capsule, nodding, egg-shaped, seeds numerous

The name coralroot refers to the knobby, coral-like appearance of the genus's rhizomes. Spotted coralroot is parasitic on soil fungi, forming mycorrhizal associations and transferring nutrients from the fungal mycelium to the orchid. Ozette coralroot, var. *ozettensis*, lacks spots on the lip and is endemic to the northwestern part of Washington's Olympic Peninsula.

Orobanchaceae—broomrape family
Castilleja hispida

harsh paintbrush

HABITAT Prairies, forest openings, lowland to mid-montane

BLOOMS Spring, summer

DESCRIPTION Herbaceous perennial, hairy, taprooted, stems several, erect, inflorescence a brushlike cluster at the stem tip, plants 8–24 in. tall

FLOWERS Bracts showy, red, orange, or yellow, hairy, lobed, lobes linear, tips rounded, sepals tubular, 2-lobed, lobes notched, petals greenish, tubular, 2-lipped, upper lip hooded, stamens 4

LEAVES Alternate, blades lance-shaped, hairy, lower leaves unlobed, upper stem leaves with 1–2 pairs of narrow side lobes, tips rounded, lower leaves smaller than upper stem leaves

FRUIT Capsule, seeds cone-shaped, tan

Harsh paintbrush hybridizes with other paintbrushes (*Castilleja* spp.) where their populations overlap. Although paintbrushes are green and photosynthesize, they also obtain nutrients from nearby plants, often grasses, a condition called hemiparasitism. Hemiparasites can survive without a host plant but are healthier with one. Harsh paintbrush is a known larval host for the rare Taylor's checkerspot butterfly.

Orobanchaceae—broomrape family
Castilleja miniata

giant red paintbrush, scarlet paintbrush, slender paintbrush

HABITAT Prairies, meadows, forests, lowland to subalpine

BLOOMS Spring, summer

DESCRIPTION Herbaceous perennial, taprooted, stems erect, often branched, inflorescence a brushlike cluster at the stem tip, plants 8–30 in. tall

FLOWERS Bracts showy, oval to egg-shaped, bright red to scarlet, rarely purplish or yellow, hairy, tips toothed or not, sepals tubular, 2-lobed, lobes toothed, tips pointed, petals greenish, 2-lipped, upper lip hooded, stamens 4

LEAVES Alternate, blades linear to lance-shaped, hairy or not, edges mostly smooth, tips pointed

FRUIT Capsule, seeds many, tiny

Giant red paintbrush has a wide ecological amplitude and is broadly distributed across the Pacific Northwest. Distinguish it from harsh paintbrush (*C. hispida*) by its larger size, fewer hairs, and the lack of lobing on leaves and bracts. Along the coast it may be confused with coast paintbrush (*C. litoralis*) that has leaning stems, wider egg-shaped leaves with rounded tips, and floral bracts with side lobes and a rounded central tip.

Orobanchaceae—broomrape family
Pedicularis groenlandica

elephant's head lousewort

HABITAT Wet meadows, seeps, streambanks, mid-montane to subalpine

BLOOMS Summer

DESCRIPTION Herbaceous perennial, nonhairy, roots fibrous, stems 1 to several, erect, unbranched, reddish, leaves fernlike, inflorescence a dense, spirelike cluster at the stem tip, plants 6–24 in. tall

FLOWERS Hoodlike, sepals tubular, 5-lobed, petals 2-lipped, pink, pinkish purple, or red, the hoodlike upper lip resembling an elephant's head, longer than the lower lip

LEAVES Basal and alternate on the stem, stalked, blades lance-shaped, 2–10 in. long, edges lobed and toothed, tips pointed

FRUIT Capsule, curved, nonhairy

Similar species little elephant's head (*P. attollens*) grows in the Oregon Cascades, the Steens Mountain area, and south into the Sierra Mountains of California. Distinguish elephant's head lousewort from little elephant's head by the relative lengths of the upper and lower petal lips. Little elephant's head has a longer lower lip compared to the upper, while in elephant's head lousewort the upper lip is longer than the lower.

Orobanchaceae—broomrape family
Pedicularis racemosa

sickletop lousewort, leafy lousewort

HABITAT Coniferous forests, dry meadows, rocky slopes, mid-montane to subalpine

BLOOMS Summer

DESCRIPTION Herbaceous perennial, nonhairy, roots fibrous, stems usually several, erect, unbranched, leafy, inflorescence an open, leafy cluster at the stem tip, with smaller, stalked clusters from the upper leaf axils, plants 6–18 in. tall

FLOWERS Hoodlike, sepals 2-lobed, petals 2-lipped, pinkish white, cream, or purple, tip of the hoodlike upper lip curled inward toward the lower lip, ½ in. long

LEAVES Alternate, blades lance-shaped, 1–3 in. long, edges toothed, tips pointed

FRUIT Capsule, curved, nonhairy

Sickletop lousewort and other *Pedicularis* species are exclusively pollinated by bumblebees, with studies showing that no seeds are produced when bumblebees are absent. Coiled-beak lousewort (*P. contorta*) flowers are similar to those of sickletop lousewort, but the plant has divided leaves and lacks leafy bracts with the flowers. The name lousewort originated from the superstition that the plant harbored lice and infected livestock that grazed nearby.

Papaveraceae—poppy family
Corydalis scouleri

Scouler's corydalis, western corydalis, Scouler's fumewort

HABITAT Forests, streambanks, coastal to lower montane slopes

BLOOMS Spring, summer

DESCRIPTION Herbaceous perennial, nonhairy, rhizomatous, stems erect, branched or not, inflorescence of narrow clusters at the stem tip or in the leaf axils, usually 15–35-flowered, plants 2–4 ft. tall

FLOWERS Spurred, showy, ¾–1½ in. long, sepals 2, ephemeral, petals 4, pale to deep pink, outer 2 lip-like, inner 2 petals shorter, fused at the tip, stamens 6, pistil 1

LEAVES Alternate, stalked, several times pinnately divided, 4 in. or more long, leaflets oval to lance-shaped

FRUIT Pod-like capsule, seeds shiny black

Seeds of Scouler's corydalis are catapulted from the plant when the mature capsule springs open, aiding seed dispersal. The similar Clackamas corydalis (*Corydalis aquae-gelidae*), rare in Washington and Oregon, has more divided, fernlike leaves, an inflorescence of 2–60 smaller flowers (¼–¾ in. long), and pink to rose-lavender petals.

Papaveraceae—poppy family
Dicentra formosa

Pacific bleeding heart

HABITAT Mesic forests, streambanks, edge habitats, lowland to mid-montane

BLOOMS Spring

DESCRIPTION Herbaceous perennial, nonhairy, rhizomatous, stems erect, inflorescence branched, 5–15-flowered, plants 6–20 in. tall

FLOWERS Heart-shaped, stalked, nodding, sepals 2, lance- to egg-shaped, to ⅛ in. long, petals 4, heart-shaped, pinkish purple, pink, or rarely creamy white, the outer pair with a short spur ⅛ in. long, the inner petals fused near the tips

LEAVES Basal leaves stalked, fernlike, blades pinnately divided, leaflets again divided and then lobed, mostly shorter than the inflorescence, stem leaves absent

FRUIT Pod, seeds shiny black

Pacific bleeding heart works well in shady woodland-style gardens. The seeds have a fleshy bit called an elaiosome, which attracts ants. The ants carry the seeds to their underground tunnels. They eat the elaiosome but not the seed, facilitating seed dispersal. Dutchman's breeches (*D. cucullaria*) can be distinguished from Pacific bleeding heart by its V-shaped flowers with long spurs and white to pale pink petals.

Phrymaceae—lopseed family
Erythranthe lewisii (*Mimulus lewisii*)

Lewis's monkeyflower, great purple monkeyflower

HABITAT Wetlands, stream edges, meadows, mid-montane to alpine

BLOOMS Summer

DESCRIPTION Herbaceous perennial, rhizomatous, glandular-hairy, stems erect, mostly unbranched, inflorescence a cluster near the stem tip, also has stalked flowers in the upper leaf axils, plants 1–3 ft. tall

FLOWERS Two-lipped, reddish pink to pink with a yellow throat, sepal tube with 5 teeth, upper petal lip 2-lobed, the lower lip 3-lobed, 1–2 in. long, stamens 4

LEAVES Opposite, not stalked, lance- to egg-shaped, 1¼–3¾ in. long, veins prominent, edges mostly toothed, tips pointed

FRUIT Capsule, seeds many

Lewis's monkeyflower is closely related to scarlet monkeyflower (*E. cardinalis*), native to southern Oregon and introduced in Washington. Although the two species can hybridize, they rarely do as scarlet monkeyflower usually grows at lower elevations than Lewis's monkeyflower. The two species have different pollinators as well, which minimizes crossing; bumblebees are pollinators for Lewis's and hummingbirds for scarlet monkeyflower.

Plantaginaceae—plantain family
Penstemon rupicola

rock penstemon, cliff beardtongue

HABITAT Cliffs, crevices, rocky slopes, lowland to mid-montane

BLOOMS Spring, summer

DESCRIPTION Subshrub, mat-forming, hairy, stems several, erect, inflorescence a few-flowered cluster at the stem tip, plants 1–6 in. tall

FLOWERS Two-lipped, pink, hot pink, or red, stalked, sepal lobes 5, hairy to glandular-hairy, petal tube wide, the upper lip 2-lobed, the lower 3-lobed, 1–1¼ in. long, stamens 5, 1 sterile, pistil 1

LEAVES Opposite, leathery, bluish green, hairy or not, blades oval to egg-shaped, ¼–½ in. long, edges smooth or toothed, tips rounded

FRUIT Capsule, seeds many

Similar species Davidson's penstemon (*P. davidsonii*) has lavender to bluish purple flowers and green rather than bluish green leaves. Another mat-forming species in southern Oregon is mountain pride (*P. newberryi*), which has magenta flowers, is usually more than 6 in. tall, and has green leaves.

Plumbaginaceae—plumbago (leadwort) family
Armeria maritima

sea thrift, sea pink

HABITAT Beaches, bluffs, rocky areas, gravelly prairies, coastal, low elevations

BLOOMS Spring, summer

DESCRIPTION Herbaceous perennial, taprooted, hairy or not, stems erect, inflorescence a dense terminal cluster with purplish bracts below, plants 4–18 in. tall

FLOWERS Funnel-shaped, stalked, sepals 5-lobed, ribbed, hairy or not, petals 5-lobed, white, pink, or lavender, tips rounded, stamens 5, styles 5

LEAVES Basal only, wiry, linear, tips pointed, 2–4 in. long

FRUIT Dry, achene-like, 1-seeded

Sea thrift has four subspecies, two of which grow in Oregon and Washington. Common and native to our region is ssp. *californica*. However, ssp. *maritima*, native to Europe and Greenland, has been found in some locations. Distinguish the two by examining the stigma (pollen-receptive area at the end of the style) in the flowers. Subspecies *maritima* has dimorphic flowers, one type with a bumpy stigma surface, the other smooth. Flowers of subspecies *californica* are one type, with bumpy stigma surfaces.

Primulaceae—primrose family
Dodecatheon hendersonii (*Primula hendersonii*)

Henderson's shooting star, mosquito bill, broadleaf shooting star

HABITAT Woodlands, prairies, rock outcrops, low elevations

BLOOMS Spring

DESCRIPTION Herbaceous perennial, roots with small bulbs, stems leafless, sparsely glandular-hairy, inflorescence a cluster of nodding, stalked flowers at the stem tip, plants 4–20 in. tall

FLOWERS Nodding, stalks sparsely glandular-hairy, sepals greenish with purplish speckles, petals 4 or 5, bent back, sword-shaped, magenta to deep pink, grading to yellow at the base, ½–1 in. long, stamens joined around the pistil

LEAVES Basal, nonhairy, stalked, egg-shaped to triangular, edges smooth, tips rounded, 1–5½ in. long

FRUIT Capsule, seeds many

Shooting star flowers nod on stalks, resembling darts, but after pollination they become erect so seed can be dispersed farther from the parent plant. In the Siskiyou Mountains and parts of California plants of Henderson's shooting star are nonhairy, have sepals without speckles, and roots without bulbs. They are sometimes grouped as var. *hansenii*.

Primulaceae—primrose family
Dodecatheon jeffreyi (*Primula jeffreyi*)

Jeffrey's shooting star, tall mountain shooting star

HABITAT Streambanks, lakeshores, bogs, meadows, mid-montane to subalpine

BLOOMS Summer

DESCRIPTION Herbaceous perennial, glandular-hairy, clump-forming, roots lack small bulbs, stem leafless, inflorescence a cluster of nodding, stalked flowers at the stem tip, plants 4–24 in. tall

FLOWERS Nodding, sepal lobes green, ¼ in. long, petals 4 or 5, bent back, sword-shaped, magenta, lavender, or rarely yellowish, grading to white with a reddish purple band at the base, ¼–1 in. long, stamens joined around the pistil

LEAVES Basal, stalked, blades lance- or spoon-shaped, edges mostly smooth, tips rounded or pointed, 2–15 in. long

FRUIT Capsule, seeds many

Jeffrey's shooting star grows in wet mountain habitats in our area, the common name shooting star referring to the flowers reminding some of a star falling from the sky. Shooting star flowers are designed to be buzz pollinated by bumblebees. The bee hangs from the stamens and vibrates its thoracic muscles, shaking pollen onto its body.

Primulaceae—primrose family
Lysimachia latifolia (*Trientalis latifolia*)

western starflower, Pacific starflower

HABITAT Forest openings, prairies, lowland to mid-montane

BLOOMS Spring, summer

DESCRIPTION Herbaceous perennial, roots with an upright tuber, stem erect, leaves in a whorl at the stem tip, the remaining leaves reduced to bracts, inflorescence a spray of pinkish flowers, each on a curved threadlike stalk, plants 4–10 in. tall

FLOWERS Star-shaped, sepals joined at the base, lobes 6 or 7, lance-shaped, petals 6 or 7, pinkish to rose, egg-shaped, overlapping, tips pointed

LEAVES Whorl of 4–8, blades oval to egg-shaped, edges smooth, tips pointed, 1–4 in. long

FRUIT Capsule, seeds many

Often found in wetter habitats is arctic starflower (*L. europaea*); distinguish it from western starflower as it has white petals, smaller leaves to 2 in. long, lower leaves that are not bractlike, and the presence of a horizontal rather than upright tuber.

Ranunculaceae—buttercup family
Aquilegia formosa

red columbine, western columbine, Sitka columbine

HABITAT Forest openings, meadows, lowland to mid-montane

BLOOMS Spring, summer

DESCRIPTION Herbaceous perennial, hairy or not, often glandular, taprooted, stems several, erect, inflorescence 1 to several stalked, nodding flowers at the stem tip and from upper leaf axils, plants 6–36 in. tall

FLOWERS Spurred, sepals 5, petal-like, pale to dark red, up to 1 in. long, spurs straight, sepal lobes lance-shaped, spreading, tips pointed, petals 5, yellow, tips rounded, stamens many

LEAVES Basal and alternate along the stem, stalked, blades palmately divided into 3 leaflets, leaflets egg-shaped, lobed, tips rounded

FRUIT Pod, glandular-hairy, ½–1 in. long, seeds several

Red columbine grows well in garden settings, preferring rich soil and partial shade. It attracts bees, butterflies, and hummingbirds. Yellow columbine (*A. flavescens*) looks similar to red columbine but has yellow flowers with curved spurs and grows primarily on talus slopes and high-mountain meadows. The two species form hybrids where their populations overlap.

Ranunculaceae—buttercup family
Thalictrum occidentale

western meadowrue

HABITAT Meadows, open slopes, forests, lowland to subalpine

BLOOMS Spring, summer

DESCRIPTION Herbaceous perennial, rhizomatous, clump-forming, separate male- and female-flowered plants, stems erect, basal leaves few, inflorescence a branched, open cluster near the stem tip, male flowers nodding, plants 1–3 ft. tall

FLOWERS Petals absent, sepals egg-shaped, green to purplish-tinged, to ⅛ in. long, shorter on female flowers than male, male flowers with 15–30 purplish dangling stamens, female flowers with spreading, purplish pistils

LEAVES Alternate on the stem, stalked, blades divided into 3 leaflets, then divided again 2 or 3 times, ultimate leaflets egg-shaped, ½–1 in. long, edges lobed, tips rounded

FRUIT Achene, oval, ribs straight, glandular, spreading in a star-like cluster

Western meadowrue is wind-pollinated, resulting in genetic exchange between clonal meadowrue clumps. Distinguish from similar species many-fruited meadowrue (*T. polycarpum*) by looking at the achene. Many-fruited meadowrue has egg-shaped, nonglandular achenes with curved, branching ribs.

Saxifragaceae—saxifrage family
Lithophragma parviflorum

small-flowered prairie star, small-flowered woodland star, small-flowered fringecup

HABITAT Prairies, coastal bluffs, balds, forest openings, lowland to mid-montane

BLOOMS Spring

DESCRIPTION Herbaceous perennial, ephemeral, glandular-hairy, rhizomatous, with bulblets among the roots, stem erect, purplish, inflorescence a cluster of 5–15 stalked, delicate flowers at the stem tip, plants 4–12 in. tall

FLOWERS Starlike, showy, sepal tube vase-shaped, 5-lobed, petals 5, pink to whitish, 3-lobed, stamens 10

LEAVES Basal and alternate along the stem, stalked, blades ½–1 in. across, divided into 3–5 leaflets, leaflets 3-lobed, stem leaves few, much smaller than the basal leaves

FRUIT Capsule, seeds many, brown, wrinkled

Similar species bulbiferous woodland star (*L. glabrum*) has 5-lobed petals, often has reddish bulblets in the leaf axils, and has minutely spiny seeds. Small-flowered prairie star blooms while soils are moist in spring and the aboveground plant parts wither after the fruit have matured. The plant lives on through its root system until spring arrives once more.

Valerianaceae—valerian family
Plectritis congesta

rosy plectritis, sea blush

HABITAT Sand dunes, prairies, bluffs, rocky slopes, lowland to mid-montane

BLOOMS Spring

DESCRIPTION Annual, mostly nonhairy, taprooted, stem erect, unbranched, basal leaves wither early, inflorescence a dense, rounded cluster at the stem tip, flowers small, fragrant, plants 3–24 in. tall

FLOWERS Two-lipped, to ¼ in. long, bright to pale pink, the upper lip 2-lobed, lower lip 3-lobed with a thick spur less than half as long as the petal tube, sepals absent, stamens 3

LEAVES Opposite, nonhairy, ¼–2¼ in. long, blades oval, egg- or spoon-shaped, edges smooth, tips rounded

FRUIT Achene, convex, ribbed at the center with winged edges

Often found growing in profusion on suitable sites, rosy plectritis is an early nectar source for bumblebees and butterflies. It grows well in sunny to partly shady gardens and may reseed year after year. If sowing seed, plant from late fall to early spring, just barely covering the seed with soil.

Blue and Violet Flowers

Asparagaceae—asparagus family
Brodiaea coronaria

harvest brodiaea, crown brodiaea

HABITAT Gravelly prairies and slopes, rocky bluffs, low elevations

BLOOMS Spring

DESCRIPTION Herbaceous perennial from a bulblike corm with a fibrous covering, stem 1, erect, leaves grass-like, inflorescence umbrella-shaped, rays of the umbel different lengths, with short bracts beneath, plants 2–10 in. tall

FLOWERS Bell-shaped, bluish purple, 1–2 in. long, 6-lobed, lobes longer than tubular portion, the outer 3 lobes narrower than the inner 3, fertile stamens 3, sterile stamens 3, longer than fertile stamens, pistil 1

LEAVES Basal only, 1–3, linear, withering before anthesis

FRUIT Capsule, seeds black

Harvest brodiaea has leaves with parallel veins and floral parts in 3s, typical of monocots. Monocots have plant embryos with 1 leaf, called a cotyledon. In Oregon, two other brodiaea species might be mistaken for harvest brodiaea: elegant brodiaea (*B. elegans*) with funnel-shaped flowers, and dwarf brodiaea (*B. terrestris*) with smaller pinkish purple flowers. They also differ from harvest brodiaea by having similar-sized sterile and fertile stamens.

Asparagaceae—asparagus family
Camassia leichtlinii

great camas, large camas

HABITAT Wet meadows, prairies, balds, lowland to mid-montane

BLOOMS Spring

DESCRIPTION Herbaceous perennial, nonhairy, ephemeral, bulb single, egg-shaped, ½–1 in. in diameter, stem 1, erect, inflorescence a narrow cluster of stalked flowers, when withering the tepals twist together covering the ovary, plants 1–3 ft. tall

FLOWERS Light to deep blue-violet or creamy white, tepals 6, equally sized, 1–1½ in. long, stamens 6, anthers yellow, stigmas 3

LEAVES Basal only, grass-like, linear to lance-shaped, to 2 ft. long, edges smooth, tips pointed

FRUIT Capsule, oval to egg-shaped, to 1 in. long, seeds black, shiny

Native Americans consider camas bulbs a treasured edible and they traditionally had a high trade value. Bulbs are cooked for many hours to increase palatability and often dried for future use. Great camas may be propagated by bulb or seed and grows well in sun to part shade in moist soils. Subspecies *leichtlinii* has creamy white flowers and is endemic to southwestern Oregon.

Asparagaceae—asparagus family
Camassia quamash

common camas, small camas

HABITAT Wet meadows, prairies, open slopes, lowland to mid-montane

BLOOMS Spring

DESCRIPTION Herbaceous perennial, nonhairy, ephemeral, with egg-shaped bulb, diameter ½–1 in., flowers stalked, clustered at the stem tip, tepals not twisting together, withering separately, plants 6–30 in. tall

FLOWERS Light blue to deep blue-violet, tepals 6, equally sized, ½–1¼ in. long, stamens 6, anthers yellow or violet, stigmas 3

LEAVES Basal only, grasslike, linear to lance-shaped, 4–24 in. long, edges smooth, tips pointed

FRUIT Capsule, oval to egg-shaped, seeds black, shiny

Bulbs of common camas are a valued Native American foodstuff. Camas bulbs are collected in summer after flowering. Common camas is quite variable with nine recognized subspecies. Distinguish it from great camas by its slightly irregular flowers, 1 tepal curving downward while the rest curve upward, and tepals often withering separately instead of twisting together. In the garden, plant it in moist soils in sunny locations.

Asteraceae—aster family
Erigeron glacialis var. *glacialis*
(*Erigeron peregrinus*)

wandering daisy, subalpine fleabane, wandering fleabane

HABITAT Meadows, streambanks, mid-montane to alpine

BLOOMS Summer

DESCRIPTION Herbaceous perennial, roots fibrous and rhizomatous, stems erect, hairy, inflorescence of 1 to a few heads at the stem tip, plants to 2 ft. tall

FLOWERS Bracts of the head linear, glandular, usually nonhairy, all about same length, to ¼ in. long, both ray and disk flowers present, rays 30–80, blue, purple, or pink, disk flowers yellow

LEAVES Basal and alternate along the stem, blades lance- to spoon-shaped, 1–6 in. long, hairy or not, edges smooth, tips pointed

FRUIT Achene, sparsely hairy, with a tuft of hair at the tip

Wandering daisy can be confused with Alice Eastwood's daisy (*E. aliceae*), a rare species in Washington found in the Olympic Mountains and present throughout the Oregon Cascades. In contrast to wandering daisy that has glandular, mostly nonhairy bracts, the floral bracts of Alice Eastwood's daisy are noticeably white-hairy.

Asteraceae—aster family
Eucephalus ledophyllus (*Aster ledophyllus*, *Doellingeria ledophylla*)

Cascade aster

HABITAT Forest openings, meadows, mid-montane to subalpine

BLOOMS Summer

DESCRIPTION Herbaceous perennial, taprooted, stems several, erect, hairy, flowers in heads, stalked, from the upper leaf axils and at the stem tip, plants 1–2½ ft. tall

FLOWERS Bracts of the head lance-shaped, in a shingled arrangement, tips pointed, both ray and disk flowers present, rays lavender to purple, ¼–¾ in. long, disk flowers yellow

LEAVES Alternate, stalkless, blades oval to lance-shaped, woolly-hairy beneath, edges smooth to few-toothed, tips pointed, 1–3 in. long

FRUIT Achene, hairy, topped by a hair tuft

Cascade aster was once part of the *Aster* genus until studies showed significant differences between North American aster species and those of Eurasia. Most North American asters have been dispersed into a number of genera, including *Eucephalus*. Only one local *Aster* species remains, alpine aster (*A. alpinus*), which also grows in Eurasia.

Asteraceae—aster family
Symphyotrichum subspicatum
(*Aster subspicatus*)

Douglas' aster

HABITAT Beaches, meadows, streambanks, disturbed areas, lowland to mid-montane

BLOOMS Summer

DESCRIPTION Herbaceous perennial, rhizomatous, stems leafy, inflorescence variable, the clusters of heads branched or unbranched, at the stem tip and from upper leaf axils, plants 1–3 ft. tall

FLOWERS Bracts of the head in a shingled arrangement, tips curved and pointed, bract base yellowish to brown, both disk and ray flowers present, rays violet, disk flowers yellow

LEAVES Alternate, those of lower stem withering early, blades lance-shaped to linear, 2–4½ in. long, edges toothed, tips pointed

FRUIT Achene, hairy, tuft of hair at top often reddish

Douglas' aster is likely the result of hybridization among several other *Symphyotrichum* species. Similar species Pacific aster (*S. chilense*), found only in coastal areas, has outer floral bracts with blunt rather than pointed tips. Douglas' aster and many others were once within a large *Aster* genus. This genus has been split into eight genera, including *Symphyotrichum*.

Boraginaceae—borage family
Mertensia paniculata

tall bluebells, tall lungwort

HABITAT Streambanks, meadows, forest edges, mid-montane to subalpine

BLOOMS Spring, summer

DESCRIPTION Herbaceous perennial, rhizomatous or not, stems several, leafy, with branched, open clusters of nodding flowers on slender stalks from the upper leaf axils, plants 6–60 in. tall

FLOWERS Bell-shaped, nodding, blue to pink, ¼–½ in. long, sepals 5, linear, hairy, petals tubular, 5-lobed, tips pointed, stamens 5, pistil 1

LEAVES Basal and alternate along the stem, stalked, basal blades heart-shaped, stem leaf blades lance- to egg-shaped, edges smooth, tips pointed

FRUIT Nutlet, wrinkled

Tall bluebells ranges from Alaska across most of Canada and dips down into the United States in the Pacific Northwest and the upper Midwest. It is shade tolerant and pollinated by bees. Like all species in the borage family, tall bluebells has a type of fruit called a nutlet, a small hard structure usually containing 1 seed. Tall bluebells would make a good addition to a meadow garden, preferring well-drained, rich soils.

Campanulaceae—harebell family
Campanula rotundifolia

Scotch bluebell, bluebell-of-Scotland, American harebell

HABITAT Meadows, rocky areas, forest openings, lowland to alpine

BLOOMS Summer

DESCRIPTION Herbaceous perennial, nonhairy to sparsely hairy, taprooted and rhizomatous, stems slender, with 3–10 stalked flowers at the stem tip, plants 4–30 in. tall

FLOWERS Bell-shaped, nodding or erect, sepal lobes linear, ¼–½ in. long, petals blue, ½–1 in. long, tube longer than the lobes, style not extending beyond the lobes

LEAVES Basal leaves stalked, blades egg- or spoon-shaped, less than 1 in. long, often withering before anthesis, stem leaves alternate, mostly linear, ½–3 in. long, edges toothed, tips pointed

FRUIT Capsule, cup- to cone-shaped, seeds brown, numerous

Slender and graceful, Scotch bluebell is circumboreal with a wide elevational range. There are several nonnative bluebell species; these have stout rather than slender stems with larger flowers. The native Scouler's bluebell (*C. scouleri*) grows in similar habitats, but its style extends well beyond the petal bell, and the petal lobes curl outward.

Fabaceae—pea family
Lathyrus japonicus

beach pea, maritime peavine

HABITAT Beaches, sand dunes, coastal, lowland

BLOOMS Spring, summer

DESCRIPTION Herbaceous perennial vine, rhizomatous, stems climbing or trailing, tendrils present at leaf tips, inflorescence of stalked, several-flowered clusters from the leaf axils, plants to 5 ft. long

FLOWERS Pea-like, 2-lipped, ½–1 in. long, reddish purple to blue, sepal tube with 5 lance-shaped teeth, style flattened, hairy on one side

LEAVES Alternate, stalked, green, blades pinnately divided into 3–6 pairs of oval leaflets, ⅓–2¾ in. long, leaf tip with tendrils

FRUIT Pod, hairy, ¾–2¾ in. long

Beach pea is found in similar habitats as gray beach pea (*L. littoralis*). Gray beach pea lacks tendrils and has densely hairy, grayish green leaves. Another maritime pea is marsh peavine (*L. palustris*). It grows on mud flats and salt marshes, and unlike the two beach peas, has stems with flattened, winged edges.

Fabaceae—pea family
Lathyrus polyphyllus

leafy pea, Oregon pea

HABITAT Forest openings, gravelly slopes, meadows, lowland to mid-montane

BLOOMS Spring, summer

DESCRIPTION Herbaceous perennial, rhizomatous, stems erect or climbing, stems leafless on lower half, tendrils present at the leaf tips, inflorescence stalked clusters of 5–13 flowers arising from the leaf axils, plants 1–3 ft. tall

FLOWERS Pea-like, 2-lipped, ½–¾ in. long, petals blue to reddish purple, sometimes white, sepal tube with 5 teeth, upper lip heart-shaped, the lower lip smaller, style flattened, hairy on one side

LEAVES Alternate, stalked, nonhairy, blades pinnately divided into 10–16 lance- to egg-shaped leaflets, 1–2 in. long, tendril present, unbranched or only forked

FRUIT Capsule, nonhairy, 1½–2¾ in. long

Lathyrus spp. flowers are designed so that pollen collects on the style hairs and transfers to the underbelly of the pollinator, often a bumblebee, as it probes the flower for nectar. The pollinator then deposits the pollen on the styles of other flowers, increasing the efficiency of pollen transfer.

Fabaceae—pea family
Lupinus latifolius

broadleaf lupine

HABITAT Prairies, forests, meadows, ridges, lowland to alpine

BLOOMS Spring, summer

DESCRIPTION Herbaceous perennial, taprooted, stems several, hairy, branched, stem branches may end in flower clusters, basal leaves mostly absent, inflorescence spire-shaped with pea-like flowers, plants 1–3 ft. tall

FLOWERS Pea-like, sepals long-hairy, 2-lobed, upper lobe wider than the lower lobe, petals 2-lipped, pale to deep blue or lavender, stamens 10

LEAVES Alternate along the stem, stalks long, blades palmately divided into 7–9 oval leaflets, 1–3 in. long, lower surface hairy, hairy or not above, edges smooth, tips pointed

FRUIT Pod, woolly-hairy, about 1 in. long, seeds 6–10

A variable species, broadleaf lupine hybridizes readily with other *Lupinus* spp. where the populations overlap. Also growing in similar habitats at low elevations are streambank lupine (*L. rivularis*) and sicklekeel lupine (*L. albicaulis*). Recognize broadleaf lupine by its wider upper sepal lobe; in the other two species the lower and upper sepal lobes are of similar widths.

Fabaceae—pea family
Lupinus polyphyllus

large-leaved lupine

HABITAT Streambanks, meadows, forests, disturbed areas, lowland to alpine

BLOOMS Spring, summer

DESCRIPTION Herbaceous perennial, taprooted or rhizomatous, stems several, hairy or not, usually unbranched, if branched the branch ends lack flower clusters, clusters spire-shaped, plants 1–5 ft. tall

FLOWERS Pea-like, to ½ in. long, sepals 2-lobed, hairy, upper sepal lobe with 2 teeth, petals 2-lipped, bluish to violet, upper lip marked with white

LEAVES Basal and alternate along the stem, stalked, blades palmately divided into 9–13 oval to lance-shaped leaflets, leaflets 1½–6 in. long, the lower surface hairy, hairy or not above, tips pointed

FRUIT Pod, curved, densely hairy, seeds 3–9

Large-leaved lupine prefers moist habitats, is tolerant of disturbance, and has several recognized varieties. Wildlife browse lupines, but they are toxic to sheep and cows. Many lupine cultivars originated from the "Russell" lupine series, hybrids developed in Britain by George Russell by crossing large-leaved lupine with yellow bush lupine (*L. arboreus*).

Gentianaceae—gentian family
Gentiana calycosa

mountain bog gentian, explorer's gentian

HABITAT Wet meadows, bogs, streambanks, subalpine to alpine

BLOOMS Summer, fall

DESCRIPTION Herbaceous perennial, nonhairy, roots fleshy, not rhizomatous, stems several, upright, unbranched, flowers usually solitary at the stem tips, plants 2–12 in. tall

FLOWERS Bell-shaped, 1–1½ in. long, with green bracts beneath, sepals and petals 5-lobed, sepals green with a purplish tinge, the lobes sometimes lacking, petals deep purplish blue streaked with green with fringed folds between the lobes, lobe tips mostly pointed, stamens 5, pistil 1

LEAVES Opposite, stalkless, egg-shaped, ⅓–1 in. long, edges smooth, tips rounded, less than twice as long as wide, basal leaves absent

FRUIT Capsule, seeds many

Distinguish from similar species King's gentian (*G. sceptrum*) and prairie gentian (*G. affinis*) as these species have leaves more than twice as long as wide and can be found at lower elevations than mountain bog gentian. King's gentian grows mostly along the coast, while prairie gentian grows in meadows and forest edges.

Iridaceae—iris family
Iris tenax

tough-leaf iris, Oregon iris

HABITAT Roadsides, meadows, open forests, lowland to mid-montane

BLOOMS Spring

DESCRIPTION Herbaceous perennial, rhizomatous, clump-forming, stems erect, unbranched, not hollow, to 1 ft. tall, shorter than the basal leaves, flowers solitary at the stem tip, rarely 2

FLOWERS Showy, sepals 3, petals 3, blue, lavender, purple, or occasionally pink, yellowish or white, sepals 2¼ in. long, egg-shaped, spreading with tips curled, edges wavy, the central patch yellow and white with darker veins, petals 2 in. long, lance-shaped, upright, edges wavy

LEAVES Basal leaves linear, ribbed, light green, tips pointed, 1¼ ft. long by ⅛ in. wide, stem leaves alternate, much shorter, 1–3 per stem

FRUIT Capsule, 1–1¼ in. long, seeds many, brown

The narrow, fibrous leaves of tough-leaf iris have long been used by Native Americans to make nets and as material for weaving. It grows well in garden settings, preferring well-drained soils in full sun to partial shade. Forms hybrids with other iris species.

Orobanchaceae—broomrape family
Aphyllon purpureum
(*Orobanche uniflora, Aphyllon uniflorum*)

naked broomrape, one-flowered broomrape

HABITAT Seeps, mossy crevices and ledges, bluffs, meadows, lowland to mid-montane

BLOOMS Spring

DESCRIPTION Annual or short-lived perennial, parasitic, glandular-hairy, nonphotosynthetic, stems short, leaves bractlike, the inflorescence one to several flowers, each single on a brownish stalk, plants 2–6 in. tall

FLOWERS Two-lipped, bluish purple, yellow, or creamy white, petal lobes 5, the edges fringed with hair, folds inside the floral tube bright yellow, sepals 5, linear with pointed tips

LEAVES Bractlike, lance-shaped, tips pointed

FRUIT Capsule, seeds many

Naked broomrape is known to be parasitic on sedums (*Sedum* spp.), saxifrages (*Saxifraga* spp.), members of the aster family, and other plants. It was long included within the *Orobanche* genus but was moved to *Aphyllon* along with other North and South American broomrape species based on DNA analysis that indicated they were different from Eurasian *Orobanche* species.

Plantaginaceae—plantain family
Collinsia parviflora

small-flowered blue-eyed Mary

HABITAT Balds, meadows, rock outcrops, forest openings, lowland to alpine

BLOOMS Spring, summer

DESCRIPTION Annual, taprooted, stems erect, flowers solitary to several from the leaf axils, plants 1½–16 in. tall

FLOWERS Two-lipped, to ¼ in. long, sepal lobes 5, petal tube bent at 45 degrees near the base, lower lip dark blue to purplish, upper lip bluish white, pink, or white, stamens 4, pistil 1

LEAVES Opposite, sometimes in whorls of 3 near the stem tip, blades oval to linear, ¼–1½ in. long, tips pointed

FRUIT Capsule, oval, seeds 2–4

Small-flowered blue-eyed Mary thrives in thin-soiled areas within a variety of habitats and blooms early in the growing season while soils are moist. It is pollinated by bees and self-pollinates as well, a trait that maximizes seed set. Large-flowered blue-eyed Mary (*C. grandiflora*) is similar in appearance but has larger flowers and a petal tube bent at 90 degrees near the base.

Plantaginaceae—plantain family
Penstemon procerus

small-flowered penstemon, pincushion penstemon

HABITAT Rocky slopes, meadows, forest openings, mid-montane to alpine

BLOOMS Spring, summer

DESCRIPTION Subshrub or herbaceous perennial, nonhairy, stems erect, usually several from a branched, woody root base, inflorescence 1 or more dense clusters in tiers at the stem tip, flowers small, plants 2–16 in. tall

FLOWERS Two-lipped, sepal lobes 5, petal tube narrow, upper lip 2-lobed, the lower 3-lobed and hairy inside, deep purplish blue, lavender, or pinkish, ⅛–⅜ in. long, stamens 5, 1 sterile

LEAVES Basal leaves stalked, present or not, stem leaves opposite, blades lance- to egg-shaped, to 3 in. long but often much shorter, nonhairy, edges smooth, tips pointed

FRUIT Capsule, seeds many

Small-flowered penstemon has several recognized varieties, with high-elevation plants often 7 in. tall or less. It makes a stunning addition to rock or meadow gardens, attracting many pollinators including hummingbirds, bees, and butterflies. Grow in sunny areas with well-drained soil.

Plantaginaceae—plantain family
Penstemon serrulatus

Cascade penstemon, coast penstemon, Cascade beardtongue

HABITAT Streambanks, draws, moist rocky slopes, lowland to subalpine

BLOOMS Spring, summer

DESCRIPTION Subshrub or herbaceous perennial, taprooted, stems erect, hairy or not, basal leaves absent, inflorescence 1 or more dense clusters at the stem tip, plants 8–27 in. tall

FLOWERS Two-lipped, sepal lobes 5, lobe edges fringed, petal tube wide, the upper lip 2-lobed, the lower 3-lobed, deep blue to purple, ½–1 in. long, stamens 5, 1 sterile

LEAVES Opposite, those on the lower stem smaller and stalked, the rest stalkless, blades lance- to egg-shaped, 1–3 in. long, edges toothed, tips pointed

FRUIT Capsule, seeds many

Penstemons have 5 stamens, but only 4 produce pollen. The 5th sterile stamen, called the staminode, often has a brushlike patch of hair along its length, leading some to refer to the genus by the name beardtongue. Studies have shown that the staminode has a function in pollination as when it is removed, fewer seeds are produced.

Polemoniaceae—phlox family
Phlox diffusa

spreading phlox

HABITAT Forest openings, rocky slopes, rock outcrops, mid-montane to alpine

BLOOMS Spring, summer

DESCRIPTION Perennial subshrub, taprooted, mat-forming, stems erect to spreading, flowers solitary at the stem tips, plants 1–4 in. tall

FLOWERS Trumpet-shaped, sepals hairy, 5-lobed, lobes linear, tips pointed, shorter than the petal tube, petal lobes 5, spreading, bluish, pinkish, or white, stamens 5

LEAVES Opposite, stalkless, blades linear, to ¾ in. long, green, nonhairy except for the cobwebby hairs on the edges near the leaf base, tips pointed

FRUIT Capsule, seeds 3

Spreading phlox brings butterflies, bees, and moths to the garden, attracted by the nectar and pollen of its flowers. Plant it in sunny areas with well-drained soil and in time it will form a low, dense groundcover covered with showy flowers.

Ranunculaceae—buttercup family
Aconitum columbianum

monkshood, Columbia monkshood

HABITAT Streambanks, wet meadows, forest openings, montane to subalpine

BLOOMS Summer

DESCRIPTION Herbaceous perennial, toxic, root tuberous, stems several, erect, inflorescence a narrow cluster of stalked flowers at the stem tips, plants 1½–6½ ft. tall

FLOWERS Hoodlike, glandular-hairy, sepals 5, deep bluish purple, occasionally white or cream, hoodlike upper sepal ¼–1 in. long, petals 2, inconspicuous, stamens many

LEAVES Alternate, those on the lower stem stalked, the upper stalkless, blade 2–7⅔ in. wide, divided into 3–5 lobes, lobes egg- to diamond-shaped, edges toothed to smooth, tips pointed

FRUIT Pod, 3–5 per flower, ¼–⅔ in. long, glandular-hairy or nonhairy, seeds ⅛ in. long

All parts of monkshood plants are considered toxic. Howell's aconite (*A. columbianum* ssp. *viviparum*), found in mid-montane habitats in Oregon and reportedly in Washington, forms bulblets in leaf axils and the inflorescence. Bulblets are a form of vegetative reproduction, plantlets that can grow into a new plant.

Ranunculaceae—buttercup family
Anemone oregana

western wood anemone, Oregon anemone

HABITAT Forest openings, coastal bogs and marshes, lowland to mid-montane

BLOOMS Spring, summer

DESCRIPTION Herbaceous perennial, hairy, rhizomatous, stem 1, erect, flowers solitary at the stem tip, plants 4–12 in. tall

FLOWERS Saucer-shaped, petals absent, sepals usually 5, showy, oblong to egg-shaped, ¼–¾ in. long, blue to purplish, sometimes white or pink, or white above and reddish purple below, stamens more than 30

LEAVES Basal and whorled on the stem, stalked, blades palmately divided into 3 leaflets, leaflets lobed and partly toothed, to 3 in. long, tips pointed, stem leafless except for a whorl of 3 leaves just below flower

FRUIT Achene, hairy

Western wood anemone has two varieties: var. *oregana*, which grows in forests and has sepals of one color, and var. *felix* (inset), which is found in bogs and marshes near the coast and has sepals that are white above and reddish purple below.

Ranunculaceae—buttercup family
Delphinium menziesii

Menzies' larkspur

HABITAT Bluffs, rock outcrops, prairies, meadows, forest openings, lowland to mid-montane

BLOOMS Spring, summer

DESCRIPTION Herbaceous perennial with tuberous roots, stem solid, inflorescence an open cluster at the stem tip, plants 4–20 in. tall

FLOWERS Spurred, stalked, spur straight, mostly ½ in. long, sepals 5, showy, hairy, bluish purple, rarely yellow, lobes spreading, tips pointed, petals 4, lower petals bluish purple, the upper often white or pale blue

LEAVES Basal leaves few, stem leaves alternate, both 2 or 3 times palmately divided, leaflets oblong, leaves stalked except for those of the upper stem

FRUIT Pod, densely hairy, seeds dark brown

Menzies' larkspur usually grows in rich soils, while similar species Nuttall's larkspur (*D. nuttallii*) grows on gravelly prairies and basalt cliffs. Sepal lobes of Menzies' larkspur are spreading, while those of Nuttall's larkspur curve inward toward the petals. Olympic larkspur (*D. glareosum*) can be distinguished by its usually hollow stems, fleshy leaves concentrated near the stem base, and (mostly) high-elevation habitats.

Violaceae—violet family
Viola adunca

early blue violet, hooked violet, western dog violet

HABITAT Meadows, forest openings, streambanks, seeps, lowland to subalpine

BLOOMS Spring, summer

DESCRIPTION Herbaceous perennial, rhizomatous, stems many, flowers solitary on stalks from the leaf axils, plants mostly less than 5 in. tall

FLOWERS Spurred, petals 5, deep blue, violet, or lavender, spur slender, often curved, half as long as the petal blades, the side petals hairy at the base, the lowest one purple-lined, stamens 5, style tip hairy

LEAVES Alternate along the stem and basal, stalked, blades heart- to egg-shaped, ¼–1 in. long, edges round-toothed, tips rounded

FRUIT Capsule, oval, seeds several

A widely distributed species, early blue violet is a larval host for several rare butterflies. Early blue violet and many other *Viola* spp. produce cleistogamous, or closed, flowers. Cleistogamous flowers are self-pollinating and resemble buds. Having both types of flowers benefits the species by ensuring seed production while retaining the adaptability conferred by genetic exchange.

Green and Brown Flowers

Aristolochiaceae—birthwort (pipevine) family
Asarum caudatum

wild ginger, long-tailed ginger

HABITAT Mesic shady forests, lowland to mid-montane

BLOOMS Spring, summer

DESCRIPTION Herbaceous perennial, rhizomatous, stems trailing, rooting at the nodes, leaves evergreen, flowers solitary at the stem tip

FLOWERS Bell-shaped, sepals petaloid, brownish purple, hairy, 3-lobed, lobes with long narrow tips, petals absent, stamens 12

LEAVES Opposite, stalked, shiny green with prominent net veining, heart-shaped, 1½–4 in. long, sparsely hairy below, usually smooth above, edges fringed with hair, tips mostly rounded

FRUIT Pod, seeds egg-shaped

Wild ginger flowers are usually tucked beneath the leaves, lying on their side near the ground. The flowers are designed to attract flies that usually feast on decomposing animals. The flies eat the pollen and carry some to the next flower. The seeds have a fleshy bit attached called an elaiosome, which attracts ants. The ants disperse the seeds by carrying them to their colonies. They eat the elaiosome but not the seed, thus effecting seed dispersal.

Liliaceae—lily family
Fritillaria affinis

checker lily, chocolate lily, mission bells, rice root

HABITAT Coastal bluffs, prairies, open slopes, forest edges and openings, lowland to mid-montane

BLOOMS Spring

DESCRIPTION Herbaceous perennial from a rounded bulb, ephemeral, nonhairy, stems erect, inflorescence 1 to several stalked flowers from the leaf axils of the upper stem, plants 6–36 in. tall

FLOWERS Bell-shaped, nodding, brownish purple to yellowish green, mottled, tepals 6, oblong to lance-shaped, ¾–1 in. long, stamens 6, styles 3

LEAVES Whorled, becoming alternate near the stem tip, blades lance-shaped, shiny green, edges smooth, tips pointed, 1–5 in. long

FRUIT Winged capsule, ¾ in. long, seeds many, brown

Another name for checker lily is rice root, referring to the small bulblets resembling grains of rice that form on the outside of the base of the main bulb. The bulblets are a form of vegetative reproduction, an alternate way the plant can produce new individuals.

Melanthiaceae—bunchflower family
Veratrum viride

green corn lily, green false hellebore

HABITAT Meadows, streambanks, bogs, forests, mid-montane to alpine

BLOOMS Summer

DESCRIPTION Herbaceous perennial, poisonous, rhizomatous, stems 1 to several, stout, erect, unbranched, leafy, inflorescence a branched, 1–2 ft. long cluster at the stem tip, branches mostly drooping, plants 3–6 ft. tall

FLOWERS Star-shaped, yellowish green to green, stalked, tepals 6, oval to lance-shaped, about ¼ in. long, outer surface densely hairy, stamens 6

LEAVES Alternate, stalkless, bright green, blades oval, 4–14 in. long, ribbed, hairy beneath, edges smooth, tips pointed

FRUIT Capsule, nonhairy

All *Veratrum* spp. are highly poisonous to humans and livestock, although some Native American communities have used small amounts of the plant for medicinal purposes. Similar species California false hellebore (*V. californicum*) has white flowers and erect to spreading flower branches. Siskiyou false hellebore (*V. insolitum*), rare in Washington but secure in Oregon, can be distinguished by its egg-shaped tepals and hairy capsules.

Orchidaceae—orchid family
Platanthera stricta (Habenaria saccata)

slender bog orchid, male habenaria

HABITAT Wet meadows, seeps, streambanks, lowland to subalpine

BLOOMS Summer

DESCRIPTION Herbaceous perennial, nonhairy, roots fibrous, stem slender, erect, inflorescence an open, leafy-bracted cluster at the stem tip, flowers fragrant but not showy, plants 6–36 in. tall

FLOWERS Hoodlike, green to yellowish green, sepals 3, the upper sepal forming part of the hood, petals 3, 2 petals curved upward, the 3rd liplike, lance-shaped, with a sac-shaped spur at the base, spur half to two-thirds as long as the lip

LEAVES Alternate, nonhairy, 1–6 in. long, blades egg- to lance-shaped, leaf tips rounded or pointed

FRUIT Capsule, oval, seeds many

Orchids have developed an effective way to transfer large quantities of pollen from one flower to another. They have structures called pollinaria that consist of 2 stalked pollen sacs connected at a sticky base. The sticky base can attach the pollinarium to visiting insects, who then unwittingly carry it to the next flower distributing the pollen.

Saxifragaceae—saxifrage family
Tolmiea menziesii

piggy-back plant, youth-on-age, bristle flower

HABITAT Forests, streambanks, trailsides, lowland to mid-montane

BLOOMS Spring, summer

DESCRIPTION Herbaceous perennial, glandular-hairy, rhizomatous, basal leaves many, stems 1 to several, erect, slender, flowers in a narrow cluster near stem tip, plants 1–2½ ft. tall

FLOWERS Tubular, sepal tube greenish purple to brown, 5-lobed, petals 4, threadlike, reddish brown, curled, stamens 3

LEAVES Basal and alternate along the stem, stalked, blades heart-shaped, 1–4 in. wide, shallowly 5–7 lobed, shiny green, sparsely short-hairy, edges toothed, tips pointed

FRUIT Capsule, seeds many

Piggy-back plant can be confused with fringecup (*Tellima grandiflora*) due to similar foliage and habitat, especially when not in flower. Tell the species apart by looking at the leaves: those of piggy-back plant are shiny and dark green, while fringecup leaves are dull green. The names piggy-back plant and youth-on-age come from small plantlets that form on top of the basal leaves. A form of vegetative reproduction, they can become a separate plant.

Typhaceae—cattail family
Typha latifolia

broadleaf cattail, common cattail

HABITAT Ponds, marshes, ditches, lakeshores, lowland to mid-montane

BLOOMS Summer

DESCRIPTION Herbaceous perennial, rhizomatous, stems erect, unbranched, flower clusters cylindric at the stem tips, the top section has only male flowers, the lower all female, plants 3–10 ft. tall

FLOWERS Tiny, male flowers wither early, exposing the stem, female flowers persistent, becoming dark velvety brown as the fruit matures

LEAVES Alternate, grasslike, blades linear, flattened, bluish green, ¼–¾ in. wide, tips pointed

FRUIT Dry, narrow, with hair tuft at the base

Broadleaf cattail grows in standing water and often forms large clonal patches. Wind pollinates the flowers and disperses the fruit. The fruit float on water, which also helps disperse seed from the parent plant. It is a key wetland plant for wildlife. The similar but nonnative species narrowleaf cattail (*T. angustifolia*) in contrast to broadleaf cattail has leaves less than ¼ in. wide and has a gap of exposed stem between the two sections of the inflorescence.

Urticaceae—nettle family
Urtica gracilis (*Urtica dioica*)

stinging nettle

HABITAT Forests, wetlands, disturbed areas, prefers rich soils, lowland to subalpine

BLOOMS Spring, summer

DESCRIPTION Herbaceous perennial with stinging hairs, rhizomatous, stems erect, unbranched, flower clusters dangling from the leaf axils, flowers male or female, on the same plant or not, female flower clusters usually near the stem tip, plants 1–3 ft. tall

FLOWERS Tiny, tepals 4, brownish, male flowers with equal-sized tepals, female flowers with 2 tepals longer than the other 2

LEAVES Opposite, stalked, blades egg-shaped, green, 2–8 in. long, edges toothed, tips pointed

FRUIT Achene, round

Stinging nettle has recently been separated into the species *U. gracilis* from *U. dioica*, which is native to Eurasia and South Africa. Genetic analysis separates the species clearly, but visible differences are minimal. One difference is the achene shape: the native species has round achenes while those of *U. dioica* are egg-shaped. The hollow hairs of stinging nettle act like a needle, dispensing chemical irritants if touched.

GOING FURTHER

This book is just an introduction to the wonders of Pacific Northwest native plants, profiling 150 of the showiest and most common wildflowers. We hope we've piqued your interest, and you'll continue exploring and learning about our native flora. There are a LOT of plants to discover here.

There are about 3700 taxa in Washington with 2662 considered native and 4866 taxa in Oregon with 3402 natives. The term "taxa" includes species plus their subspecies and varieties. These plants include what we usually think of as wildflowers, plus trees, shrubs, grasses and grasslike plants, ferns, and aquatics.

You could easily spend a lifetime studying our native flora and never see and learn all the plants. We have each dedicated decades to traveling around our region exploring for plants. Each year we encounter plants that are new to us as we travel to places that we hadn't previously visited. As you further your study of our flora, you'll want to consult other more comprehensive books and make use of online references. Here are some of our favorites that we consult.

Books: Field Guides

We're a bit prejudiced, but these comprehensive books from Timber Press have sold thousands of copies and have become dog-eared and well used by plant lovers throughout the Northwest:

- *Wildflowers of the Pacific Northwest,*
  Mark Turner and Phyllis Gustafson, 2006.

- *Trees and Shrubs of the Pacific Northwest*, Mark Turner and Ellen Kuhlmann, 2014.
- *Weeds of the Pacific Northwest*, Mark Turner and Sami Gray, 2024.

If you're looking for more of a natural history approach in a book that includes plants, animals, fungi, geology, and climate we recommend another book published by Timber Press: *Natural History of the Pacific Northwest Mountains*, Daniel Mathews, 2017.

Along with many of our plant-loving friends, we often carry one of these books from Lone Pine Publishing when we're out in the field. These volumes include a bit of ethnobotany for many of the plants they cover:

- *Plants of the Pacific Northwest Coast*, Jim Pojar and Andy MacKinnon, 2016.
- *Plants of Southern Interior British Columbia and the Inland Northwest*, Roberta Parish, Ray Coupé, and Dennis Lloyd, 1996.
- *Alpine Plants of the Northwest, Wyoming to Alaska,* Jim Pojar and Andy MacKinnon, 2013.
- *Wild Berries of Washington and Oregon*, T. Abe Lloyd and Fiona Hamersley Chambers, 2014.

Books: Technical References

Botanical technical references can be intimidating, even for experienced users. It takes time and practice to learn to use a dichotomous key as you carefully examine often-obscure details of a plant. You'll likely make good use of your hand lens as you hone your observation skills. But these books are the standard references used by professional botanists (and field guide authors):

- *Flora of the Pacific Northwest: An Illustrated Manual.* Second Edition. C. Leo Hitchcock and Arthur Cronquist, edited by David E. Giblin, Ben S. Legler, Peter F. Zika, and Richard G. Olmstead. University of Washington Press, 2018.
- *Vascular Plants of the Pacific Northwest*. C. Leo Hitchcock, Arthur Cronquist, Marion Ownbey, and J. W. Thompson. Five volumes. University of Washington Press, 1955–1969.
- *Flora of Oregon*. Stephen C. Meyers, Thea Jaster, Katie E. Mitchell, Linda K. Hardison. Three volumes. Botanical Research Institute of Texas Press, 2015–2025.

If you're on the northern or southern edge of our territory, the technical manuals for British Columbia and California can be useful:

- *Illustrated Flora of British Columbia*. G. W. Douglas, et al., editors. Eight volumes. Crown Publishers, King's Printer for British Columbia, 1998–2002.
- *The Jepson Manual: Vascular Plants of California.* Bruce G. Baldwin, et al., editors. University of California Press, 2012.

Smartphone Apps

Books can get heavy in your pack, and you probably carry a smartphone with you most of the time. While we haven't gotten to the point of having a plug-in DNA analyzer for our phones, these first two apps can substitute for a field guide. They include simplified keys, multiple photos for most plants, descriptive text, and distribution maps. Both of these are self-contained and once downloaded do not require an internet connection:

- *Oregon WildFlowers: A Guide to the Wildflowers, Shrubs, and Vines of Oregon*. Oregon Flora Project, Botany and Plant Pathology Department, Oregon State University, and High Country Apps, LLC. 2014 (and regularly updated).
- *Washington WildFlowers: A Guide to the Wildflowers, Shrubs, and Vines of Washington and Surrounding Areas*. University of Washington, Burke Museum, and High Country Apps, LLC. 2013 (and regularly updated).

Many people are looking for the easy way out: an app that will identify a plant just from a picture. While this technology is getting better each year, it's still prone to making incorrect identifications. Sometimes they get it right and sometimes they don't. You'll probably want to confirm what an auto-identification app is suggesting by consulting another source if you're concerned about accuracy.

- Apple's *Visual Look Up*, in iOS 15 or later on iPhones and newer iPads, uses Siri to attempt to identify plants, dog breeds, and landmarks. It needs an internet connection and doesn't work with all photos.

- *Google Lens* is in the camera app of select Android devices and is also available to download for other Android devices and iPhones. It requires an internet connection to work.
- *iNaturalist* is much more than just an app. It's available for Apple and Android, as well as the web browser on your laptop or desktop computer. To use it, you upload one or more photos of a plant (or other organism), and the software attempts to identify it based on thousands of other photos that have been identified by experts. Photos you upload are added to the database, contributing to citizen science worldwide. You can also use iNaturalist to search for specific plants and see where they've been found by other users.
- *Seek by iNaturalist* identifies plants, wildlife, and fungi. This app, available for Android and Apple, draws on observations submitted to iNaturalist.org and partner sites, and identified by the iNaturalist community. It requires an internet connection to work.

Websites

Websites can be a better source of up-to-date information about plants, particularly currently accepted names, since they can be updated relatively easily and frequently compared to books that are expensive and time-consuming to revise and print. Most of the websites we suggest include plant photos as well as current taxonomic details.

- **Burke Herbarium Image Collection:** burkeherbarium.org/imagecollection. Developed and maintained by the University of Washington Herbarium at the Burke

Museum, the site has over 3200 vascular plant species with photos. It includes a simplified key as well as several ways to search the collection.

- **OregonFlora:** oregonflora.org. OregonFlora is based at the OSU Herbarium at Oregon State University. The site is comprehensive for Oregon's plants and includes simplified keys, search functions, and a mapping tool to identify plants found within an area.
- **CalFlora:** calflora.org. CalFlora is run by a nonprofit set up to provide the service, which includes data and photos for all of California's flora (some of which is also found in Oregon and Washington), along with extensive search and mapping tools. CalFlora links to CalPhotos (calphotos.berkeley.edu), a collection of about 800,000 photos (and growing) of plants, animals, fossils, people, and landscapes from around the world.
- **E-Flora BC (Electronic Atlas of the Flora of British Columbia):** linnet.geog.ubc.ca/biodiversity/eflora. E-Flora BC comes from the University of British Columbia. It includes all the plants considered to be part of the flora of British Columbia and some plants from adjacent areas. Included are species descriptions and illustrations from the eight-volume *Illustrated Flora of British Columbia* and interactive maps showing where the species have been found.
- **Pacific Northwest Wildflowers:** pnwflowers.com. This website from Mark Turner, one of the authors of this book and three other printed field guides, houses a collection of over 16,000 plant photos and a searchable database that accesses the descriptions and distribution maps from *Wildflowers of the Pacific Northwest*.

- **Flora of North America:** floranorthamerica.org. This site is the online version of the thirty-volume *Flora of North America* and includes all the text from those volumes as well as some updates since the books were printed. You can browse by family or genus or search for a plant if you know its name.

- **USDA PLANTS Database:** plants.sc.egov.usda.gov/home. The PLANTS Database provides standardized information about the vascular plants, mosses, liverworts, hornworts, and lichens of the United States and its territories. It's searchable in several ways and maps plant distributions by state (and in some cases, by county).

- **Plants of the World Online (POWO):** powo.science.kew.org. This site, from the Royal Botanical Gardens, Kew, is a great resource for finding the currently accepted name for a plant. It includes some photos and maps distribution at the state or provincial level.

- **Ecoregions of North America:** epa.gov/eco-research/ecoregions-north-america. This is the site from which we drew the information in the ecoregions section of the climate and habitat chapter of this book.

There are many other websites dedicated to plant identification, but the ones we've listed are the ones we consult routinely when we find a plant new to us or want to check distribution data.

GLOSSARY

achene. Small, dry fruit, containing one seed.

alkaloids. Water-insoluble, nitrogen-containing compounds that often exhibit pharmacological action, such as nicotine.

alpine. Found above timberline at high altitude.

alternate. Arranged singly at different heights along the stem.

annual. Plant that germinates, flowers, sets seed, and dies in one year.

anther. Pollen-producing segment of the stamen.

appressed. Lying flat against another organ, as hairs pressed against the surface of a leaf or stem.

aquatic. Growing in or on water, floating or rooted to soil at the bottom with submerged stems or shoots.

ascending. Curving or angling upward from the base.

axil. The upper angle between the leaf and the stem.

bald. Thin-soiled treeless habitat in an otherwise forested area, usually characterized by seasonal drought and ephemeral species.

basal. Found at or near the base of a plant or plant part.

berry. Fleshy fruit with more than one seed within the soft tissue.

biennial. Plant completing its life cycle in two years.

bisexual. Having functional male and female reproductive structures.

blade. The expanded part of the leaf.

bract. Leaflike structure, usually associated with the inflorescence, but also sometimes on the stem.

branch. Secondary stem, growing from main stem.

bristle. 1. Large stiff straight hair. 2. Aster family, fine hairs at top of flower arising from inferior ovary.

bulb. An underground bud, enlarged for nutritive storage from which stems and roots are formed.

bulblet. A small bulb, associated with the root or stem system.

capsule. Dry, many-seeded fruit.

caudex. Persistent base of an herbaceous perennial.

circumboreal. Located or distributed around the world at northern latitudes.

deciduous. Quality or characteristic of something being shed or discarded seasonally.

disk. In the aster family, the part of the head made up of disk flowers.

disk flower. Flower in the aster family with a regular, tubular shape, rayless.

egg-shaped. Leaf blade wider on one end and narrower at the other.

elaiosome. Fleshy structure attached to the outside of a seed.

endemic. Limited to a certain geographic or edaphic area.

ephemeral. Lasting for a short period of time.

erect. Upright from the ground.

evergreen. Living through one or more cycle of seasons, as in evergreen leaves. *See also* deciduous.

extirpated. No longer in existence in a particular region, but still living in other areas of the world.

fibrous root. Type of root system with all root branches the same width or thickness.

fleshy. Thick, juicy as in many plants in the sedum family.

fruit. Any ripened ovary and associated structures containing the seed(s).

fused. United, as petals to sepals or petals, sepals to each other, not free.

genus. Taxonomic rank smaller than a family and greater than the species level. Plural genera.

glabrous. Smooth, without hairs.

gland. Small, round body that emits a sticky substance, sessile on outer plant surface or on end of a hair.

hair. Thin to thick threadlike growth on outer surface.

head. Dense collection of sessile or nearly sessile flowers making up the inflorescence. Often said of members of the aster family.

hybrid. Plant created when two different species interbreed.

inflorescence. The arrangement of the flowers, or cluster of flowers of a plant.

leaflet. Portion of a divided or compound leaf blade.

linear. Narrow with parallel sides.

lip. Upper or lower section of an unequal corolla or calyx.

lithosol. Type of shallow soil with hard rock underneath.

lobe. A subdivided segment of an organ. The free parts of a flower tube.

native. Growing in place without human aid or actions.

nut. A hard, dry fruit containing a single seed.

nutlet. Small fruit, looks like a nut, usually one of several.

oblong. Longer than wide, rounded.

opposite. Arranged in pairs at same level, and on opposite sides, often said of leaves on the stem.

oval. An ellipse.

ovary. The organ that contains the ovules, usually develops into the fruit after fertilization. The wide portion of the pistil.

palmate. Divided from a single point and radiating around it.

parasite. Plant that receives part or all of its nutrition from another organism.

perennial. Plant living longer than two years.

persistent. Remaining attached, not falling off plant for some time.

petal. Member or segment of the corolla, the inner perianth whorl, often colored.

pinnate. Divided into leaflets arranged on opposite sides of an axis.

pistil. Female reproductive organ of a plant, usually consisting of an ovary, style, and stigma.

prickle. A sharp growth, thorn, or spine, usually restricted to smaller growths.

ray. Strap-shaped petal of a flower in the aster family or a stalk of an umbel inflorescence.

ray flower. Aster family flower with one long strap-shaped petal, often with three lobes.

rhizomatous. Plant that has rhizomes.

rhizome. A horizontal stem below the ground that sends off rootlets and vertical stems or leaves.

root. Structure from base of stem, usually underground. Anchors the plant and absorbs minerals and water.

root crown. Area of root where the stems are formed.

rosette. Cluster of leaves at ground level, usually in a circle.

seed. Plant embryo, usually packaged with starchy, nutritive tissue and surrounded by a protective coating.

sepal. A fused or free member of the calyx, usually green and bractlike.

serpentine. Common term for rock or soil high in magnesium and heavy metals such as chromium and nickel and low in calcium. Often has specialized flora.

shrub. Woody plant that usually has several main stems, or is branched from the base.

spine. Stiff, slender, sharply pointed structure.

spreading. Held outward from point of attachment.

spur. Hollow, usually rounded projection from petal or sepal, containing nectar.

stalk. Secondary stem, often referring to structure supporting a flower or leaf blade.

stamen. Male reproductive organ bearing pollen composed of a stalk (filament) and pollen sacs (anther).

staminode. Modified stamen that does not produce pollen.

stem. The central support of a plant bearing the other organs, such as leaves and flowers, usually aboveground.

stigma. Part of the pistil where pollen may attach.

stipule. Appendage at base of a leafstalk, generally paired, variable in form, often leaflike, sometimes scalelike or a spine.

stolon. Runner, an elongated stem lying on the ground, forms new roots and stems.

stoloniferous. Plant that has stolons.

style. Usually slender portion of the pistil connecting the ovary and the stigma.

subalpine. Just below timberline.

subshrub. Plant with woody tissue only near the base of stems and in the root system.

talus. Mass of medium- to large-sized rock fragments at the base of a cliff.

taproot. A larger main root from which smaller root branches are formed.

teeth. Alternating projections and indentations on the margin or edge.

tendril. Slender twining or coiling structure, by which a climbing plant grasps for support.

tepal. An undifferentiated petal and/or sepal, in which sepals and petals look the same.

throat. The expanded opening of flowers with fused sepals or petals.

tube. Fused sepals or petals forming a cylindrical structure.

tuft. Cluster of something such as hair, leaves, or flowers growing from a common point.

umbel. Inflorescence with three or more stalks radiating from a common point.

unisexual. Having either male or female reproductive structures.

vein. Vessels by which water and nutrients are transported. Often easily seen in leaves.

vernal. Pertaining to spring.

vine. Trailing or climbing plant with a long, flexible stem and often supporting itself by use of tendrils.

INDEX

Mark Turner has more than thirty years of experience photographing garden and native plants for books and magazines. He brings the eye of an artist together with the mind of a botanist to create clear, high-content photographs that enable viewers to learn about and understand the characteristics of the plants he photographs. Mark is a past board member of the Washington Native Plant Society and maintains a website about Pacific Northwest wildflowers (pnwflowers.com). He is also a well-regarded speaker on the garden club and native plant circuit and gives workshops on both plants and photography. Mark lives in Bellingham, Washington.

© Brian Turner

Ellen Kuhlmann is a professional botanist with extensive experience with Northwest flora. She has a background in fire ecology, rare plant research, and plant community ecology. She worked for the US Forest Service for many years, and for six years was the project manager for Seeds of Success, Washington Rare Plant Care and Conservation (Rare Care), a program sponsored by the Royal Botanic Gardens, Kew. Ellen lives in Bellingham, Washington.

© Mark Turner